# Career ♥
## ♥ Cupid

WRITING
ON STONE
PRESS

Your Guide to Landing and Loving Your Dream Job

# Career Cupid

by
CHRISTINE FADER

Writing on Stone Press Inc.

© Writing on Stone Press Inc & Christine Fader, 2009

Library and Archives Canada Cataloguing in Publication

Fader, Christine, 1969-
    Career cupid : your guide to landing and loving your dream job / by Christine Fader.

ISBN 978-0-9811529-0-5

    1. Job hunting.  2. Career development.  I. Title.

HF5381.F229 2009        650.14        C2009-900591-3

Artwork and Cover Design: Joanne Howard, Small Dog Design
Illustration: Barbara Johnson and Lee Howard
Interior Design and Layout: Charlotte Westbrook Wilson

*Top 10 Reasons to Quit Your Job*, page 87
Used with permission
www.Salary.com

## WRITING ON STONE PRESS

Writing on Stone Press Inc.
957 Gilroy Crescent
Coquitlam
British Columbia V3J 3S9
www.writingonstone.ca
info@writingonstone.ca

*For Michael, my Happily Ever After at home*

# Contents

Introduction — 9

### I. Career Dating – *Why finding your dream job is like dating*

1. Finding your dream job — 13
2. Why great women choose bad work — 17
3. First love with a side dish of platitudes — 23
4. Wishing upon a star — 27
5. Channelling your Hootchie Mama groove — 31
6. Does this skirt make me look fat? — 37

### II. Diving into the Job Dating Pool – *On the way to your dream job*

7. One-night stands, transition jobs and other "dating" decisions — 49
8. Why can't I meet any "nice" jobs?! — 57
9. Ready, set . . . his parents! — 61
10. Proposals, prenuptials and job offers — 69

### III. Landing your Dream Job – *And living happily ever after at work*

11. When good women go baggy — 77
12. Your cheatin' heart — 83
13. Sex isn't everything but . . . — 89
14. The seven-year itch — 93
15. Heeding the call of Career Cupid — 97

### IV. Lipstick, Business Letters and Other Tools of the Trade – *Useful information for your journey to Happily Ever After*

16. I need a vacation when . . . — 105
17. Test your dress code savvy – Answers — 107
18. Speed dating cheat sheet — 111

Acknowledgments — 113
About the Author — 115

# Introduction

How many times has the sentence, "Wow, I just didn't get any sleep last night because that job search book I'm reading was so engrossing!" crossed your lips? Uh huh. I thought so.

Let's face it, most of us are going to need a job at some point to survive and many of us are dreaming about finding and growing old with a job we'll really love. Like romantic relationships, we often wish our career relationships would combine stability with excitement, romance with dependability and we would be thrilled if we could find a job that would keep the career romance alive over the long term. In other words, we want Happily Ever After at work. But how do we find it? Many people rely on parents or friends to help them figure out this stuff. Often, this guidance is well meaning but outdated or not helpful because the advice-giver may be a bit of a stranger to happily ever after at work too. Many people have, in fact, given up on the pursuit of this contented state.

Just because divorce seems to be running rampant through the Western world doesn't mean you should give up on the idea of happily ever after – in relationships or your career. But let's be honest here. There's a bigger barrier. How exciting is it to learn about career and job search? In my work as a university career counsellor and college instructor over the past ten years, I have noticed that there are lots of career books on the market but they are not very fun to read.

So…let me "edu-tain" you. And hopefully, you'll learn some things along the way without feeling as if you're getting your legs waxed very slowly and badly. Whether you're reading this book because you're desperate to leave an unhappy place in your career or you're just wondering if there's something better out there for you, you'll gain some ideas that will help you move forward. There's nothing worse than feeling ho-hum about your career. Well, okay, there are some worse things like famine, war, disease, death and over-tweezed eyebrows. With all these atrocities going on, it's even more important to grab the life victories we can, like finding career happiness. And frankly, I think women are inherently deserving of the possibility of happily ever after at work just on the basis of having to deal with PMS for a big chunk of their lives.

# ♥ Career Cupid ♥

As you may have guessed by now, this book is aimed at women, but if you're not a woman and you're reading this, there's useful stuff in here for you too. For example, you might know some women who would find this info helpful – and here's the great part – you could score serious points by giving them a book like this. Or, you might be getting in touch with your feminine side. I'm all for that and I'm happy to have you tag along. If the girlie cover offends you, just buy a handy dandy book cover in something more your style. May I suggest corduroy?

This book also makes a great gift for high school, college and university women and, in a pinch, can double as a handy seat, rain shelter or weapon against suspected household intruders, even though it's really just the furnace making that scary noise.

*Christine Fader*

# Career Dating

Why finding your Dream Job is like Dating

♥ *Chapter 1* ♥

# *Finding your Dream Job*

My first job was working as a temporary secretary for two weeks in the maintenance department of a large local factory. I was 17 years old and happened to be employed during the factory's annual shut down, which meant that I and the 50 or so men in the maintenance department were pretty much the only people wandering the halls. While at first I kept a fairly steady eye on all available exits, I soon became one of the gang and spent the rest of my time there learning – mostly about what I liked in a job and what I didn't like.

> **Lesson 1** When you're really shy and have a phobia about using the telephone, it's probably best not to accept a job that requires you to staff a phone with eight incoming lines and 32 pagers. Luckily, I managed not to faint when they showed me the phone system. (Note to hopeful career changers in the audience: fainting doesn't make the best first impression.)
>
> **Lesson 2** People fall over themselves when they see (or hear) how quickly I type. Seriously – my typing speed is like some kind of freaky gift. (Note to self: find more work where I can get undying adulation!)
>
> **Lesson 3** Never, ever, ever eat the food from the vending machine down a dark hallway beside the employee washrooms. Actually, in retrospect, the proximity to the washrooms was a wise plan. The "Salisbury steak", on the other hand, probably wasn't.

Armed with these few experiential lessons and some youthful enthusiasm, I puffed up my hair (it was the 1980s), put a shiny new penny in each of my pseudo-silver snakeskin penny loafers, and set about finding my next position. I had started career dating.

♥ ♥ ♥

Like finding a great relationship, career dating can start with playing the field. See what options are out there. See what drives you crazy and what makes your heart beat faster with excitement. If you went straight from school to long-term work, perhaps you didn't get to sow your career wild oats. You might be thinking, "What if I settled? What if

## ♥ Career Cupid ♥

there's something better out there for me and I missed it?" Maybe you were sensible but you gave up trying to shoot for career bliss. You looked at your options (and your impending car payment) and thought, "I'd be stupid to turn down this job. So what if it's not 'the one'. It's a good job and I'd be an idiot (and even more debt-ridden) if I let it pass me by."

What you did was choose the rock-solid guy . . . but not the one who made you weak at the knees. And I'm not criticizing your decision – because I've done it myself. Your current job might be one of the relationships you had to go through before finding "the one". What if you could have both stability AND passion at work?

I believe that in the same way that many women yearn for a great romantic relationship (I know it's old-fashioned to state that out loud but I think it still holds true, no matter how "modern" the woman), they are also eager to find a great career romance. They crave authenticity at work, a place to feel connected and valued and kind of jelly-like from the sheer joy that comes from working at something you love. Many women seem to want help to make the right match in their work lives: a career love affair that will last a lifetime or at least a couple of decades! They are seeking work that is fulfilling and makes them feel as if they were put on this earth for a great reason. Sure, we get all that from other parts of our lives too – but wouldn't it be great if the time we spent at work (2000-plus hours every year for most of us!) was spent doing something that kept us awake some nights because we were so excited about it? What a change that would be from losing sleep worrying about the next personality altercation, or how to get 75 hours of work done in a 40-hour week, or gnashing our teeth about how mismanaged, abandoned and unappreciated we feel. And hey, more smiling means fewer of the I-hate-my-life wrinkles and more of the I've-got-a-great-secret-joy-that-comes-from-inside-of-me-and-makes-me-beautiful wrinkles. Let's face it, if we have to have wrinkles (and how not to have them is a whole other book), then I know you're probably agreeing with me about which type you'd rather have!

♥   ♥   ♥

I use the analogy of careers and dating because, just like dating, career management is a process. It's a process that most human beings have to go through (except perhaps Paris Hilton and she has a whole bunch of other issues to contend with) and like relationships, sometimes it's fun, sometimes it's awful, but a lot of the time the whole thing is kind of a mystery that we just do our best to navigate. We haven't really been taught HOW to find great work – we just know that we NEED to find a job. So we blunder around and do the best we can. Some people strike

# ♥ Chapter 1 ♥

career gold but many people spend their prime earning years living for weekends and holidays. Despite the lack of a perfect fit at work, it's not necessarily all doom and gloom. Hopefully our hearts don't get trampled on too many times, hopefully we don't drain our bank accounts too often, but we still seem to search fruitlessly for that elusive prize: dream job = happiness.

Many people are spending their days on earth trying to find happiness. I certainly am! It takes different forms for different people, of course (I myself have been known to dance a goofy, happy dance just because I found a great pair of daisy-patterned rubber boots!) but given that many of us spend a lot of time working, we want to find at least some of our happiness in the career part of our lives. Providing the bills are getting paid, for many people, the goal is to find something they love to do. We've all heard about lottery winners who don't quit their jobs even though they no longer need a pay check. That's usually the sign of a person who has found her career passion. It doesn't take money to keep her coming in day after day. She does it for the sheer joy of being able to be involved in something that has meaning and gives her something back. How cool would that be? Okay, kinda supremely weird, but cool!

But how do we find a passion like that? That's what this book is about. The first step in the process, like finding a long-lasting relationship, is partaking in a little dating. Dating helps you find out what's "out there". Dating allows you to try without the buy. It also involves knowing something about yourself and what you're going after. We'll talk more about that later.

You may remember dating as something that was really fun or you may have a bit of nervousness about it. Both can be expected while career dating as well. Maybe you're not 17 years old like I was when I started career dating. Maybe you've been out of the career-dating game for a while. Perhaps you've been in a long-term relationship with a job that once felt exciting but lately has grown rather predictable and even annoying. Maybe you're even thinking about cheating! Dating your way to the career romance you've dreamed of might be a great strategy for you. But before you can start dating, we need to rehash some possibly painful old history in the next chapter: *Why Great Women Choose Bad Work*.

♥ **Chapter 2** ♥

# Why great women choose bad work

Trisha, a friend of mine (I've changed her name so she won't ban me from her next margarita party) has a terrible pattern in her life. She's a great woman but she consistently winds up with some guy who thinks that it's cool for him to generate no income, lie on the couch all day and yell at her rudely to bring him beer after beer from the fridge. Somehow, her initial excitement at meeting "the one" always seems to culminate in her fetching stuff for an ungrateful, nasty guy on her couch. And even though he may look different (her current guy has more hair than the previous one), it's as if she just dressed up the same old guy in different hair.

Many of us do the same thing with our careers. We're unhappy with what we're doing so we take a deep breath and we leap somewhere else. A few months or a couple of years down the road, we realize that we've ended up with the same old job with different hair. So we try again and again. But despite putting our hearts, our courage and our security on the line time and time again, somehow we never seem to find our dream job. Just like I wonder if my friend Trisha will ever find her dream guy (although I wish she would because I want my friends to be happy), I wonder if it's possible to go a whole career and never find the job that really makes your heart sing. What am I saying? Of course it's possible! Still, there are examples everywhere of great women who chose bad work.

Why do we do it? Well, if you're like me (or my friend Trish), you probably have lots of very valid reasons. Here are some of the (very valid) but still problematic "reasons" (excuses) I've used in the past. Some of them may ring a bell with you.

### At least it's familiar . . .

Just like women who get caught up in the "I've known him since high school" trap when they're dating, we succumb to the old velvet-lined rut. Staying with a job that's familiar to us – even if it's not particularly fulfilling or what we want from our lives. How can we resist the pull of a place that we know – and better yet, that knows us? It's a job that saw us through pregnancy, the loss of a parent and that thankfully brief spell

# ♥ Career Cupid ♥

when we gained 35 pounds. We have friends there and have built up the middle-class Holy Grail: "pensionable time"! How can we just ditch all that history and go looking for something new and scary?!

Don't get me wrong. Familiar can be good. Familiar is probably the right place to be if you're in a bit of a "coasting" phase of your life. If you have more than four major stressors in your home life, then you might need to be in a "coasting" phase where you don't add more pressure to your life by shaking up your career in a major way. I use four as a somewhat arbitrary number since it's the number I know I can cope with before I find myself driving almost daily through the nearest Dairy Queen for a Chocolate Extreme Blizzard on the way home from work. But I have friends who have eight or twelve stressors and can handle them beautifully without even reaching for their under-eye concealer. Your stressors might include trying to get pregnant or adopt, trying to decide whether you should get pregnant or adopt, trying not to be pregnant, raising children, dealing with an acutely or chronically ill family member, assisting aging parents, going through a bad breakup, finishing or returning to school, trying to ignore an unhappy marriage, trying to find someone who will call you for a second date, trying to get little Beatrice to stop cutting her bangs with her kindergarten paper scissors, or any combination of these and more. On the other hand, shaking up your career might be the glimmer of hope you've been waiting for to distract you from all the other sludge you have going on in your life. You can decide. Whatever you decide, keep or find people in your life who will cheer you on and cheer you up.

**It was right there in the want ads . . .**
I know people who have successfully met the partner of their dreams at a bar. But that doesn't mean I think that heading for the tequila shooters and Frankie Goes to Hollywood music is the best strategy for finding the partner of your dreams. The same principle applies to finding your ideal job. Looking in the want ads is one place to start but the chances of your perfect match just floating by when you happen to be looking are not that high. For one thing, only around 20 percent of work is advertised. That leaves a whopping 80 percent of work that is hidden from the wandering Internet spiders* and newsprint reams. However, many people continue to look for their dream job solely by scouring the want ads. The old advice is annoying but accurate: You can't keep doing the same things and expect different results.

Also, have you ever noticed that when you see a product on a shelf, all prettied up and on sale, you suddenly feel that you really want it

---

*Software programs that "crawl" around and search the Internet.

# ♥ Chapter 2 ♥

(even though you weren't even thinking about it half an hour ago)? And, have you ever noticed that sometimes when you get said item home you leave it in the bag and sort of stuff it under the corner of a chair for ages until you finally stumble upon it as you're vacuuming because your mother is coming over. Not only that, do you have a hard time remembering exactly why you wanted it in the first place? Beware the abyss masquerading as job ads. They can distract you from your real goal: finding work that YOU CHOOSE AND LOVE.

**He seemed like such a nice guy . . .**
When my friend Trish has cried on my shoulder over the years about her lack of success finding the guy she dreams about, I have asked her, "What's your dream guy like?" She often responds with some variation of, "Well y'know – nice guy, romantic, good job, nice butt of course – someone who understands me." She's just described everyone and no one in a sentence. And women wonder why guys can't figure them out?!

I think that in romance and career management, you have to be SPECIFIC. Otherwise, how will you recognize the right match when it comes along? I don't want to sound too clinical about all this – I mean, I get the importance of chemistry – but I also know that we have whole hosts of things that can muck up a good thing when it comes along and we also have whole hosts of things that can make a mucky thing look good when really…it's just a guy with different hair who will end up lying on our couch yelling at us rudely to fetch stuff.

Trish needed to refine her "perfect guy" wish list to something much more useful that she could refer to when she felt muddled by the great car her latest suitor was driving (she's got a weakness for large, old man cars). So we took each item on her too-general list and broke it down. For example, what did she mean by a "nice guy"? At first, she struggled and came up with additional generic descriptions like "sweet" and "sensitive" but then I asked her to give me an example that would SHOW her that someone was a "nice guy". She said, "If he said please and thank you all the time to me and other people, it would show me he's a nice guy." Once we hit that specific mark, there was no stopping her and she was able to come up with additional PUT YOUR MONEY WHERE YOUR MOUTH IS statements that, to her, said someone was a "nice guy". We moved on to "romantic". In the swing of things now, she started off easily with, "Well, if he brought me flowers once every few weeks for no special reason, it would be romantic."

And so we continued down her wish list and created a new, much more Trish-specific and evidence-based list. Just like Trish, in order to end up with something better in your career, you need to start with a

# ♥ Career Cupid ♥

very specific wish list. This wish list should contain concrete information and it should be WRITTEN DOWN. We'll talk about how to do this later. This is a personal document so don't worry about your spelling or how silly anything sounds. Whether you write it in lipstick on a serviette or in your best calligraphy, put it somewhere you can find it and refer to it often. You'll need it when you are feeling stuck, uninspired or when those annoying, self-righteous people in your life say things like, "So…what job are you not leaving this week?"

**I would be a quitter if I left . . .**

The end of that sentence is usually . . . "so I'll stay but complain a lot." This excuse is really common. I think it comes from fear and it usually leads to one thing – we turn into bitter women! We wander around, our mouths pursed in huge perma-frowns. We're so unhappy we could scream but instead of letting loose, we just feel angry and depressed and trapped and sometimes that unhappiness leaks out on to the people around us. If you find yourself frequently lashing out in a voice that sounds remarkably like that judge from American Idol, your current relationship may not be right for you.

It happens in relationships and it happens in work. I'm all for commitment but I don't define commitment as simply staying put when the going gets rough. I think it means that you have to be actively working at something, putting positive energy into it. Simply hanging around grumbling is not about loyalty or commitment. It's about martyrdom (and no, that's not the new stiletto heel). It's about fear. That's when people become ghosts of themselves, wandering through their days, not really giving their all anymore. They're too tired, too overworked, bored, bitter, unappreciated or burned out to be able to even step outside themselves for a minute. By this point, they have a hard time seeing how much wrong they're doing to themselves. They have definitely moved way past being able to see how much wrong they're doing to others. Usually at this point they've also stopped brushing their hair because they just . . . can't . . . be . . . bothered. It's tragic really.

It's important to be ethical and know when you are no longer putting in as much as you're getting out. How will you know when enough's enough? You may not. That's why my advice is to work on the "I need a vacation when . . ." sheet at the end of this book. You need to write this down BEFORE you get to "enough is enough" because by the time you get there, chances are you won't be able to see it or worse, you will rationalize it to yourself and anyone else who will listen. If you're even thinking, "I've just about had it with this job", then it's more than time to start making some changes. If you're already there, it's okay. You can still

♥ Chapter 2 ♥

fill out the "I know I need a vacation when . . . " sheet as a get-out-of-jail free card in the event of future breakdowns.

**Someone else would kill to have this great job . . .**
Near the inevitable end of their tenure, my friend Trish's guys would often say, "You know, there are plenty of other women who would love to be with a guy like me."

You may be looking around and thinking that other people look happy doing this work. Acquaintances might say things like, "Wow, what a great job you have! You're really lucky!" For a time, these reassurances might help sustain you. But it also makes you a passive victim of your circumstances. You're succumbing to something because it was the path of least resistance and it seems to be a popular and envied position. Like Trish, however, you may eventually grow strong enough in your spirit to know that while those statements may be true, it still doesn't mean that it's the right place for you. The rude guy on the couch CAN be ousted little by little from your career life. He may look perfectly lovely on someone else's couch. This is where your written, accessible wish list comes in handy. Refer to it as often as you need to. It will help you focus and remind you that your unique dreams and aspirations are worth pursuing. And you are responsible for going after them.

♥ *Chapter 3* ♥

# *First love with a side dish of platitudes*

**There may be a broken heart involved**
Just like first love, the first significant career relationship you have can be wonderful . . . and it can sometimes lead to what feels like an irreparably broken heart. Not everyone crashes and burns of course. I do know of people who met their career or romantic soul mate at the tender age of 15 and lived Happily Ever After, but that's not reality for most of us. It's probably a good thing, too or I would now be living in England in a two-bed semi with a guy whose marriage role models call their wives "the old trout".

If you're suffering from a career broken heart because of a less-than-stellar experience with your first, second or fifteenth career romance, fear not. You can still find career happiness. Warning: this is the part where I say things that sound trite and patronizing but which, unfortunately, are true.

**There are more fish in the sea**
If you're weeping into your non-fat, triple foam extravaganza morning after morning, try to remember that it is quite common not to find Happily Ever After on the first go out of the gate. After all, you're new at this career relationship thing and you may have leaped at the first job with a nice butt that walked by. Or maybe it was a job that didn't even have a nice butt since you desperately needed something to pay for that luxury they call rent and food.

But even though "nice butt" or "no butt" job wasn't right for you in the end, it wasn't a total loss. In every career relationship, you contribute skills and you learn skills. You also gain information that will help you refine your wish list. Perhaps you used to think that a nice butt was a priority for you. Turns out that it might be lower on the list now, having been replaced by the item: "looks me in the eyes and not at my chest when talking to me". Or, you might have learned that nice butt is still important to you but in order to also get "looks me in the eyes", you need more education or experience or to work in a different role.

Even though it hurts like the first time you waxed your bikini line, you will come out the other side of your first career romance. It may take time and you may need to coast a while in something that doesn't risk

23

♥ *Career Cupid* ♥

trampling your heart as much. Just like in romance, you may need a "transition guy" job to help you through the bumps (or rent payments). But as the tired old saying goes: there are more fish in the sea, so keep fishing, you brave woman, until you find the right species for you (I prefer scallops myself). Each fish you pull out of the ocean will give you more information about what you're looking for and what you want to throw back.

**We need to talk**
No, in this case, YOU need to talk. If you're feeling disillusioned, depressed or wishing you had a one-way ticket to Fargo, North Dakota, it's time to rally the troops. Don't suffer in silence. After all, misery loves company, right? All I ask of you is that you make some of the talking and venting you do a little bit productive. Every unhappy woman should be allowed some time living in her pyjamas, consoling herself with bad daytime television and a jar of Nutella eaten with a spoon. Try to move through that phase quickly and into spending time ranting to your friends and having coffee dates where the theme of the conversation seems to be "why me?". Feel free to indulge yourself in the obligatory "I deserve it" purchase of something you didn't need.

But at some point, try as hard as you can to talk about what's next. Try to focus your thinking towards your next goal and what it's going to be, rather than dwelling on your present or past yucky circumstances. What can YOU do to change things? Maybe you change your outlook, your job or you change your mind about what your dream job looks like. But something's got to give. If it doesn't, you'll be stuck in doldrums-ville for ages – and that only leads to bad things like getting drunk at the employee golf tournament and confessing loudly that you killed all your evil coworker's plants by feeding them a daily dose of diet Mountain Dew.

**No one is perfect**
Remember when you could sprawl out on your big bed and pull all the covers out and wrap yourself up in them like a cocoon? And now you have to fight for one small corner of the bed surface and you wake up in the middle of the night with your bed partner snuggled up with all the covers and your bare bottom chilling in the breeze? This is relationship compromise. You probably won't leave your man because of it, but it's not…perfect and sometimes at 3:17 a.m. when you're feeling sleepy and over-exposed, you kind of wish it was.

Part of finding career Happily Ever After is learning, sometimes painfully, that every job – even the craziest, incredibly perfect for you one – will have its warts. Many jobs will encroach on your ideal way of

♥ Chapter 3 ♥

doing things and necessitate some changes in your lifestyle. Most jobs demand that you not only show up at a specific time, but actively participate in the events that are happening while you're there. Yes, that means even when you're hung over, tired, grumpy, premenstrual or just "not into it". Some jobs even try to demand pieces of your integrity, your ethics or your beliefs. It's up to you to learn and decide the balance with which you can live.

Many people complain of feeling disillusioned when they enter their "real" career. If you feel that your idealistic and hopeful edges are being sanded off one day at a time by the realities of work, try to live in denial for a while (after all, I've heard that it ain't just a river). In addition to allowing you to earn essential and desirable income, any work has value if you put your best into it – even if you have a difficult time knowing exactly how you're going to make it look like something fabulous on your résumé. That's not just my Anglo-Saxon Protestant work ethic talking. I'm sure you've heard the expression, "No experience = no job", right? Employers like to hire people who have worked before (even in unpaid or unrelated work). So feel good about any experience you are socking away. Just like your first love, you may experience moments of euphoria and times when it will really feel awful. Look at it as a kind of happily-ever-after rite of passage that will help you get to future great stuff.

If you're seriously unhappy, read the chapter on divorce. It's not the least painful solution, but it may be the right one to get you out of this funk and back in your happy place.

**It's not you, it's them**
You've heard it. Maybe you've even said it. You're breaking up with or being broken up with and the classic words are uttered: "It's not you. It's me." There are career relationships that will just not be right for you – even though they might be perfectly wonderful for someone else. The trick is to try not to extrapolate your bad experience to EVERY job out there. Just as the loser man with whom you've wasted the last three years of your life does not represent how every guy will behave, one job is not the same as the next – even if they're in the same field. Be careful to avoid creeping cynicism. You are powerful, invincible and all that stuff. As the song says, "You are Woman." Let's hear you roar!

# ♥ Chapter 4 ♥
# Wishing upon a star

My husband and I shop for groceries completely differently. When I shop (which, I freely admit, is rarely), I wander the aisles, leisurely picking up items and dreaming about what I could do with them. Would this whatchamacallit root from the exotic vegetable bin taste good with sweet red peppers? If I buy this hunk of Havarti, could I make something fabulous with it?

My husband, on the other hand, spends time even before leaving for the store, to go through the flyers and see what's on sale. He makes a list of the items we normally buy and clips coupons from the flyers for them. He keeps a running tab on what's in our freezer and baking cabinet and makes lists as we run out of things. When we get to the store, he assigns duties with all the precision of his military background: "How about you go fetch the naan bread and the bagels in aisle three and I'll head over to aisle seven and get apples and bananas?"

There's no wandering, no dreaming, no ending up with a bunch of food in the fridge that goes with nothing else and ends up being wasted. I really admire that. Left to his devices, however, we would eat the same ten things year in and year out.

Over time, I've learned that I can do my part by understanding that ingredients get used more if I have a recipe that uses them (and since that time I made lasagna but forgot to put in the noodles, I've given up on ever being a domestic diva who can just wing it). He's learned that occasionally we can buy something spontaneously . . . *even if it's not on sale!* We've both learned that we each have a role to play in the shopping formula. When we combine our skills, we end up with a pretty good balance of efficiency AND variety in our grocery-shopping strategy.

The grocery-shopping story is my long-winded way of trying to get you to think about your information-gathering style. That's because this chapter is all about getting information collected about your WISH LIST. It is really, really tempting to want to rush right into career dating so you can get to the grand prize = dream job soon! However, just like rushing into romantic dating, it works better if you know a few things about what you're going after first.

# ♥ Career Cupid ♥

It's helpful if you understand whether you gather information methodically using tools like lists or whether you prefer to gather it intuitively with flashes of insight. I'll be frank when I tell you that it's a little bit easier to write advice for the list maker because I can simply say, "do this or do that" and they will follow the instructions to accomplish the goal. They love having a procedure to follow. Those of you who gather information more like me, will find those rules chafing and may even get downright rebellious when asked to make or follow a list. So how do we get you to gather information? I'm going to try to do it experientially since you tend to like to be in the moment to gather information. I'll admit that there is kind of a list involved at the end but that's just the very last bit and will hopefully be quite painless by that point.

**For the list makers**
You may be eagerly awaiting the list-making challenge. All you probably need is a bit of direction about how to construct your list. I already know it will be a thing of beauty because you're great at this kind of thing. So my only advice for you is to be as honest as you can, be as specific as you can and don't get so caught up in the fun of list-making that you forget the object of this whole exercise, which is to find out what your dream job looks like. Still, don't forget to put on your résumé that you're great at prioritizing and making lists!

**For the rebels**
Unlike your list-loving counterparts, you have probably considered skipping this whole chapter. If you've stayed out of sheer curiosity (even with the overwhelming sense of dread you feel), try this more intuitive method of information-gathering instead. Fetch your favourite beverage. Put on some comfy clothes. Some people find it helpful to talk through this stuff out loud to another person so phone someone or invite someone over to help you. Get some great snacks and then revel in the blast from the past you are about to experience.

**For everyone**
Think about career relationships you've had in the past. Even if you're embarking on your first "real" job, you may have had work-type experiences that were volunteer, extra-curricular or even working for your dad. Each one of those experiences has the ability to give you information about what you love to do, what you don't love so much and what you outright hate to do. They can also help you understand HOW you prefer to work. Maybe that torrential rain-filled summer of tree planting tells you that even in the worst weather you love working outdoors and according to a goal or quota.

♥ Chapter 4 ♥

Take out your résumé, if you have one. If you don't, you'll need to write down a quick list of every job, volunteer job, extra-curricular activity and educational experience you have had. Look at each item one-by-one on your résumé.

If you're a list-maker, make a list with three columns labeled: tasks I loved and want to do again; tasks that I can take or leave; tasks I hated and never want to do again as long as I live.

If you're a rebel, think about (or tell your friend about) the best, most fun work you ever did. Have a pen and paper or some kind of recording device handy to capture the information. Then think about the work you hated the most and why. Tell them all the hilarious and inspirational stories that go with these experiences. You know you want to! After all, for people like you, the facts themselves are not the most interesting part – it's the interpretation, patterns and meanings connected to those facts. Interpret your findings (or have your friend interpret them). What does it tell you about yourself and your goals?

**Are you stuck?**
When constructing your wish list, get inspiration from it by thinking about your activities, environments and outcomes.

*Activities: If I could do any activity at all at work, I would*
- Read romance novels all day
- Work with flowers
- Make elderly people happy
- Sing Simon and Garfunkel songs
- Shop for shoes
- Organize bits of data

Now it's your turn. Write down or talk about as many things as you can. Don't censor yourself. Try to think of all kinds of activities that you just love doing. Don't worry about whether they make sense logically or if you can get paid to do them.

*Environments: I work best in places*
- Where people are happy
- Where things around me are beautiful and stylish
- Where the atmosphere is supportive and friendly
- Outdoors
- With powerful people

# ♥ Career Cupid ♥

Now it's your turn again. (Hint: If you can't think of items, try to remember places you've worked that DIDN'T seem right. Often your best environments are the opposite of the worst ones).

**Outcomes: I feel most rewarded when**

- I get paid well
- I helped someone feel better
- I have seen something to its successful conclusion

You probably have more than one answer here again. Try to prioritize from MOST rewarding to LEAST rewarding.

Once you have a master page of items, you can start to pare it down. The dream job wish list comprises mostly the things from the "I love to do this" part of your list or experiences. Think of it like constructing your wish list for your ideal man. You probably won't get absolutely everything on the list, but you need the information to help you have a tangible goal to aim for and so you can recognize it when it floats by looking all twinkly and sexy. Your wish list will probably evolve as time goes on and as you take jobs and leave jobs and learn what schmucks to avoid. Remember when you thought that all you really wanted in your happily-ever-after guy was a hot car and a great smile? Your dream job ideal will probably also become more refined (okay, picky!) over time. You will change too, so keep your wish list going and updated as much as you can. Each time you take a career leap of faith, it will help you. As long as you fulfill enough wishes from your wish list with each step to feel shivery with excitement for the next job, you're on your way to getting ever closer to your Happily Ever After at work.

# Chapter 5
# Channelling your Hootchie Mama groove

I love watching the Food Network. As I mentioned in the last chapter, ever since I forgot to put noodles in the lasagna I was making for when my parents were coming for dinner, I've pretty much given up on being a "natural". Actually, I'm so far from a "natural" that I actually forgot to put the noodles in the lasagna TWICE. Yep, all that cheese-and-sauce layering threw me right off.

Think of this whole quest for a dream job thing as part-recipe, part-treasure hunt. Once again, the similarities with finding romantic Happily Ever After abound. Sometimes, when you're looking for "Mr Right" or even "Mr Right Now", you start with a dating website. But unlike going to an Internet job board, if you're on a dating website, one of the first things you tend to do is fill out a bit of a profile of yourself.

It's only natural that to find a good match "out there", you have to know something about and, more importantly, be able to tell other people something about yourself. This is how we end up with statements like the following:

> "Curvy Scooter Girl seeks Pirate Gentleman with zest for life (and Cabernet Sauvignon) and love of opinionated women."

Each word is laden with meaning and innuendo and choosing them can be excruciating! How can you sum yourself up in such a short space and ensure that you will attract the right kinds of matches? We all know there are nice guys out there in cyberspace but there are also creepazoids. How do we write a profile that will attract the right ones? This is the challenge. Despite this, millions of us pony up our creative writing skills and money in order to get started on the quest for romantic happiness.

Yet, when it comes to career happiness, looking at ourselves is often the last thing we want to think about. For some reason, we don't go through this same self-reflection process when we approach a job search board. Why? We talk a lot about the terrible or dull or "just not quite right" jobs we have had but we dive back out there again at the first sign of a job posting, never stopping to think about the other part of the equation – ourselves!

# ♥ Career Cupid ♥

Try to start thinking about job search as a dating website. For one thing, if it's anything like a dating website, you might be inspired to log in regularly to tweak your profile and see if anyone has said hello. This is a good thing! The more visible you are to employers, the better.

Like a dating website, there are loads of great jobs in the masses of entries, but how do you find the ones that are right for you? I encourage you to do the same thing you would do in your search for a dream romance. One crucial step is to work on your profile. Think about yourself. Every profile has two parts – the part about you and the part about what you're looking for. You may have already started thinking about what you're looking for if you've begun your wish list. Now it's time to think about the "you" part.

**Got the T-shirt**
Some people approach this process based on past experience. You tried for a job but it didn't work out. They never called you after you worked for hours on your résumé or you thought you'd aced the interview. The experience wounded you in ways you don't care to repeat. You might be tempted to start your career self-profile with a list of skills, qualifications or barriers that are blocking you from getting to your career. But this is focusing on the wrong end of the equation again. This is like saying "Curvy scooter girl seeks guy who's not going to expect her to do dishes". Plus, it doesn't help you ensure that "curvy scooter girl" is actually the final and public definition of yourself that you want to show to the world.

**The kissing savant**
I remember after a period of dissatisfying relationships and a particularly devastating break-up, I sat down one evening and wrote out a list of what I was looking for in a partner. It felt sort of ridiculous at the time because…well, I felt like I was making a shopping list to take to Boys 'R Us.

- Pair of twinkly eyes
- Smile that makes my knees melt
- Great spontaneous and willing kisser (face-cupping while kissing a definite bonus).

But not yet having discovered the mythical "man store", I had no idea where I would find someone who fit the description I had written out. I ignored that nasty voice and I put the list under my pillow (it was sort of the modern-day version of fruitcake) and slept on it.

## Chapter 5

When I woke up the next morning with my usual bad hair and my list plastered to my cheek with drool, I had a revelation.

I realized that I had a tendency, like many women, to ignore major parts of my own personality and interests in order to mould more seamlessly (I called it "being supportive") to a guy. In that very solitary yet empowering moment as a single woman, I knew that I was missing half the information if I only focused on what I wanted. I also needed to have something I could refer back to, that was about me, when I found a match. It was a kind of touchstone for me – a reminder of who I really was so I could avoid swaying too far from my own truth, even in the face of a kissing savant face-cupper with twinkles.

So along with my "ideal man" wish list, I also wrote out a description of who I was, what great qualities I had and what was important to me. Mine was entitled, "Don't forget this stuff – even when you become a spineless jellyfish girl in love." You can call yours whatever you want. The point is that I believe this same process works and is essential for increasing the odds that you'll find Happily Ever After at work.

**Think: Hootchie Mama**

So be selfish for a while. I know it's not easy since many women are used to thinking about everyone but themselves. Try to stick to thinking about yourself. You need a statement about yourself that will not only put you on the market but will help you find the sexiest, most interesting and fun work out there that matches you. We'll call this your "Hootchie Mama" statement. So, what is it that makes you who you are? What are you really good at? What's the descriptive statement or (eek) tombstone inscription that will sum up your talents and personality?

> "Creative organizer with mechanical engineering design expertise and a passion for golf seeks..."

Not interesting enough for you? Fair enough. As you write your own thoughts down, try to use your imagination. Be bold! This is the time to sell yourself and your incredible gifts! Think of it as flaunting your assets in your favourite outfit. Don't limit yourself to what you've already done or been in your career. Think about what you know are your truths and talents . . . who you are and what you do, when qualifications and what people think aren't part of the equation.

One of the keys to this exercise is to try not to worry about whether there actually is any job that will match your talents. If you get caught up in the practicalities of finding the work (if it even exists), then you'll stunt your self-reflection process (not to mention your Hootchie Mama

❤ *Career Cupid* ❤

flow and we just got that going!). Just try to write down your gifts and talents as they have meaning for you now.

If you're one of the mass majority that has many more truths and talents than can be summed up in one statement then, lucky you. Although it can feel overwhelming, the good news is that you probably have many career options where at least some of your unique qualities and passions will be supported. Just like the woman who finds a man who fulfills her need for adventure, it's great if he can also fulfill her need for peace and solitude. But to find this, it helps if she first knows that she needs adventure and peace and solitude to be her happy, authentic self. You increase the happily-ever-after quotient by moving towards work that "braids" or blends a few of your truths together.

Going back to the romance example, you're great at listening but you also tell great stories at parties. You have the ability to wear exuberant clothing gracefully and work creative magic in your kitchen.

If you can find a guy who supports or at least doesn't interfere with a couple of these items, that's great. If you can find a guy who matches some or all of them, it might be even better. The same goes for career search.

**The mirror has many faces**
If you're stuck, it's time to call in reinforcements. You know how your friends can help you decide if that dress you're trying on makes you look more like Dudley Moore than Demi Moore? They can also help you remember the best parts of yourself. They know who you are and how you tick. Sometimes you are so close to yourself that it's hard to articulate what's really great about you and what you want to preserve or grow into. Often it's incredibly obvious to your friends because they have consoled you, admired you and sometimes even envied your unique character traits for years.

This is not the time to scoff when your friend tells you for the umpteenth time, "I've always told you that you are really creative/analytical/great with numbers . . . ". Listen to what they have to say and why they are saying it. There are often good clues in that information about the things you spend a lot of time thinking about or doing. These could be the seeds of a dream job.

**With these layers, I thee wed**
My lasagna was pretty soupy and hard to eat without the noodles and your search for Happily Ever After at work will fall flat too without some substance to it. Armed with your wish list AND your Hootchie Mama groove (even if they're only works in progress), you can start career dating. And once you start career dating, you can begin to find the

# Chapter 5

places where your Hootchie Mama statement:

> "Creative organizer with mechanical engineering design expertise and a passion for golf . . . "

will connect with your wish list:

> " . . . seeks golf course design firm in the Washington area"

The good news is that the layers of this particular lasagna come from you. You have built some of them already and you'll continue to build them. The trick is to pay attention to them and keep listening and adding to them. Because at the end of the day, there are a lot of cheese-and-sauce jobs out there to distract you.

♥ *Chapter 6* ♥

# *Does this skirt make me look fat?*

Remember how you pulled everything out of your closet for your first (and second and third) date with Mr Wonderful? The same rules apply with career dating. Whether you're ready to start Speed Dating, a One-night Stand or to meet Transition Guy or the Job of Your Dreams, before you make that first contact, it's important to think about how you will present yourself.

**What to do about Aunt Martha's chin?**
You can't do anything about inheriting Aunt Martha's chin, so make the most of your presentation. That said, dressing for an interview is all about looking as if you fit the work and that what you wear is not distracting from the most important part of the interview – what you say. Avoid over-focusing on the wardrobe part of the process (and Aunt Martha's chin) and instead be prepared to talk honestly and with evidence about your experiences. You want people to think, "Gee, what a great employee this person could become", not, "Gee, what a great outfit!".

**It's not you, it's me**
If you want to avoid flashbacks to a bad date you had and this famous brush-off line, think about the details. Now I know I just advised you to avoid over-focusing on your wardrobe, but let's get real here. Would you date someone who looked dirty and smelled bad? You know . . . when it's not a Saturday night and your judgment is, shall we say, somewhat blurry? Interviews are like first dates. You can make or break your chances in the first ten seconds – and that means you need to spend some time thinking about the details.

**It's not rocket science**
I know you're smart enough to figure this out but I'm compelled to review it because I still see people making mistakes when they come to interviews or go to meet with employers. To present a positive, competent image, you want to have clean hair, clothes and teeth, be well-pressed and have no inappropriate body parts showing. It may seem obvious, but make sure that your belly, toes and cleavage are

# ♥ Career Cupid ♥

covered. (You're right; I don't think Pamela Anderson has read this book.) Be careful when you cross your legs, that listeners are not distracted by the sight of your skirt rising up a bit too high. Wear skirts that are no shorter than knee-length and, if wearing trousers, that your socks are long enough to create a seamless band of colour from your trouser hems down to your carefully polished shoes. All of these little details will help ensure that people are riveted by what you are saying and not distracted by what you look like. On the other hand, if you're going for a job interview at somewhere like MTV, then you should probably call Pamela for some pointers about what to wear. I'll be no help.

**I feel pretty, oh so pretty**
Okay, so you may not want to feel like Maria in *West Side Story*, but wear something you feel good in. With the general basics from above in mind, wear something that helps you project yourself positively. Most candidates attending a job-related meeting (even a One-night Stand) wear something that looks like a suit, however, it is not always necessary. Depending on the work, a shirt or blouse and dressier pants or skirt will do just fine. Focus on looking competent, clean and tidy. If wearing a suit makes you feel unnatural or stiff, you will not present yourself as authentically and positively, so choose something else – as long as it fits the work environment. Keep in mind that if you are faced with a waiting room full of people wearing suits and you are not, you may feel a bit goofy.

**To know me is to love me**
Wear new or borrowed clothes around the house a bit first. You look great when you stare in the mirror, but tear yourself away and try these things before you leave for your interview: sit down and stand up a few times. Are the clothes too big or too small? Do the buttons gape? Can you undo the jacket without fumbling? Do the shoes squeak? If you are wearing heels, do they promote a competent and comfortable image or do you look as if you're going out to a party? Do the colours you're wearing make your face look energized or tired? Hint: Although many candidates wear navy, black or grey, choose colours that help you feel and look your best. With all the fashion decisions you have to make, it may be a good plan to keep your most successful friend on speed dial, in case you need advice.

**Hello, I'm Chanel No. 5 and you are . . . ?**
If your perfume is arriving ahead of you, chances are you have already made a fatal mistake. In all professional conversations, it is best to avoid

## Chapter 6

perfume or body sprays completely. It is especially important these days since many workplaces now have fragrance-free policies. Many people are sensitive or even seriously allergic to perfumes so, although it may be tempting to splash on some of your favourite fragrance when you get dressed up, leave it at home this time. That said, deodorant is . . . ahem . . . still a must-have.

**Preparation checklist**
If you have enough notice about an interview, try the following preparation checklist:

| Task | Timeframe | Done |
|---|---|---|
| Buy or borrow something to wear | 1–2 weeks ahead | |
| Bond with it: try it on and wear it around the house for an hour | 1–2 weeks ahead | |
| Check hems, collars and armpits for cleanliness, wear and loose threads | 1–2 weeks ahead | |
| Check to ensure socks/hosiery are appropriate, clean and in good repair | 1–2 weeks ahead | |
| Make any adjustments/alterations necessary | 1 week ahead | |
| Wash/dry clean and iron your items | 2 days ahead | |
| Remove price tag from bottom of new shoes, polish old ones | 2 days ahead | |
| Clean your teeth, comb hair | On the day | |
| AVOID cologne | On the day | |
| Dress for interview, remove lint | On the day | |
| Practise sitting down | On the day | |
| Have someone admire you and wish you "good luck"! | On the day | |

♥ *Career Cupid* ♥

**What do they mean by "business casual"?**
There are three general categories of workplace dress: business, business casual and casual. As with dating, a good rule to follow is to dress for the guy you WANT, not the guy you HAVE. If you dress on a day-to-day basis for the job you're going after, you have a better chance of looking like you will fit it once you get there.

Please note that the information here consists of general guidelines only. That's because general guidelines are always better than a dictatorship and they're easier to read than pages and pages of details. Plus, I am not a fashionista. Try the Yellow Pages. I bet you'll find plenty of fashionista wannabes just dying to give you advice.

**Business**
Business dress is commonly found in corporate types of environments such as banks and financial services companies.

- Business dress is usually comprised of a matched suit. The suit can be either a skirt suit or a pantsuit. Wear what feels most comfortable for you.

- Wear a shirt or blouse with a collar. It is usually best to wear a solid colour or a small pattern as opposed to something large and potentially distracting to the eye.

- Darker colours tend to look more formal, however, you should wear colours that suit you and make your feel good. Think – what would I wear to make my ex's new wife jealous? . . . But dial down the eagerness by about 20 percent.

**Business casual**
Business casual is the most common workplace dress in North America today. However, because it includes such a broad range of choices, it can be tricky. Not as tricky as figuring out what your husband, boyfriend or teenage son is thinking, but still, pretty tricky.

Choose this category for any interview that is not in an extremely corporate environment. Even if you are going for a job where the dress code is usually a uniform or very casual, it's best to wear business casual to the interview.

- Business casual is a broad category. At the top end (corporate business casual), you might wear a suit; however, it need not be matched (for example, you could wear a grey jacket with black dress pants or skirt).

- A more casual level of this category includes shirt or blouse and

### Chapter 6

skirt or dress pants. You could also wear a sweater with dress pants/skirt.

- You may want to wear the upper end of business casual. This allows you to look professional, yet should the work environment be unexpectedly casual you can remove the jacket and look instantly dressed-down.

- Going to a career fair? Many career fair exhibitors are corporate companies, so corporate business casual may be most appropriate. Check the company website for information if you are unsure.

**Casual**
It might sound uptight, but it is probably wise to bump your wardrobe up to business casual any time you are going to meet with an employer. It shows that you are taking the conversation and the work seriously and can even help you look more competent and authoritative. Consider giving up your favourite flip-flops for the day. It might be worth it! Once you have the job and if the workplace is casual, you can choose from this category.

- Casual dress for the workplace includes casual pants and skirts, shirts (with or without a collar).

- T-shirts without logos or sayings are appropriate.

- In many workplaces, clean and tidy jeans may be acceptable. Try to avoid the dreaded tapered-leg jeans. They only make you look like you're shaped like an ice cream cone from the waist down.

**Tattoos, piercings and other forms of self-expression**
You may be expecting this section to tell you to remove, change or otherwise hide your various kinds of body art. Not so. The first thing you have to do is decide how much of your personal identity and expression you're willing to compromise in order to get a job. It's okay to adjust your stand on this over time. You may find that your lip ring and flaming motorcycle neck tattoo are well accepted by employers.

**The rule of cats in the shower**
I used to have a cat that absolutely loved water. I'd just barely hop out of the shower and he was right in there, rolling himself around in the last bits of water sitting in the corners of the tub. It just goes to show that although most cats dislike water, there are some who really do like it. It's the same with employers and their take on tattoos and piercings. So, how will you know whether the employers you meet are shower-loving cats or not?

41

# ♥ Career Cupid ♥

One clue would be that you're getting meetings or interviews and then no call-backs. In some cases, this can be a hint that something is happening in the interview. One possibility might be that the employer is too distracted by the sight of your piercing and tattoo to remember to offer you a job. If that is the case, then it's time to reassess your look and decide whether you are willing to do anything to change it in order to better connect with the employers you are meeting. Or, consider looking for jobs in environments that are less conservative (hint: work environments such as mainstream customer service are not usually very open-minded).

The bottom line is that you do need to think about your audience. Remember the golden rule – dress to fit the work you want + 10 percent. Look around the place you want to work. How do people dress? If you're going for a job in a hip music store, you don't want to look really conservative. Likewise, you may want to tone down your wicked orange 'do' for that job as an interior designer with the most prestigious firm in town.

**Strategies for downplaying body art:**

- Wear extremely small and discreet facial jewellery
- Remove facial jewellery for the day of the interview and on the days when you work
- Cover up body art with clothing or make-up.

**What to bring and who not to bring**
If you're in the midst of job searching, you may want to collect together a sort of kit that you can grab in a hurry when you're called for an interview or go to apply for a job. Consider including:

- Two or three pens (leave the Sponge Bob pen for writing letters to your ex that you never send)
- Pad of paper
- List of questions you have for the employer
- Directions to the employer's location
- A few copies of your résumé
- Names and contact info for references
- Reference letters, if you have them
- Transcripts or a typed list of your courses and marks

- Cell phone (good for emergencies, but keep it turned off)
- Tissues
- Brush, comb or other implements of hairstyling
- Lucky rabbit's foot or other comforting talisman.

**Is that a Kate Spade bag or are you just happy to see me?**
Once you have all your stuff collected for the meeting with an employer, you need a place to put it. The first thing to remember is less is more. Carry only one thing and it will leave you a hand free to able to do things like open doors and participate in the North American customary handshake.

As for the bag itself, choose something that can hold all your stuff but isn't too large. Choose something in reasonable repair and that won't leap out visually and say, "Hey, look at me, I'm a neon yellow bag!" In other words, choose something that adds to your interview look without overpowering it. Many women choose a slim binder, covered clipboard or laptop case.

**Don't miss this great deal for the low, low price of $29.95**
Okay, so you're not selling your skills like a cheesy late-night infomercial, but you still need some promotional materials. Some people choose to bring a portfolio/binder with a few examples of their previous work (e.g. that nifty newsletter you produced while working as a member of the Parent-Teacher Association).

**Delivery in 30 minutes or it's free**
I belong to a network of career counsellors and recruiters and sometimes you hear some pretty wacky stories about what candidates do in interviews. Among the strangest I've heard is the story of a recruiter who was interviewing a candidate when there was a knock on the door, announcing, "Pizza delivery". The interviewer looked up, bewildered, from her list of questions, just in time to see the candidate jump up and open the door. "Oh, here's my lunch," he declared as he paid the delivery fee. Seeing the interviewer's outraged expression at this inappropriate situation, he suddenly paused and said, "Oh, sorry, did you want a piece?"

The moral of the story is, of course, to eat before or after you go to an interview and not DURING it. Unless the employer specifically invites you for a meal, they'll want to focus the time they spend with you on talking about the work, not watching you chew. The same rule goes for

♥ *Career Cupid* ♥

gum or candy. Leave them for another time so the employer doesn't get an involuntary and memorable view of your tonsils.

It is acceptable to bring an individual container of water with you. When you're nervous, your throat will often get dry and water can help you pause appropriately to collect your thoughts and take a drink. It's not messy if it spills and it's usually not offensive to anyone.

**Last but not least**
I hesitated to write this, but it does happen, so I can't leave it out. If you've never even considered doing this, then I hope you'll be amused rather than insulted by Jin's story below – because you are obviously on the right track. If you've done this, suffice it to say that if you're old enough to earn money, you need to learn that – just like *American Idol*, this is a gig that requires you to step up to the spotlight on your own. Leave the friends, parents and other curious onlookers at home. If you have a well-meaning, but over-zealous parent, child, sister or friend wanting to join you at an interview or discussion with your boss, leave this passage lying open somewhere really conspicuous. I recommend the bathroom.

**The story of Jin**
Twenty-three year old graduate student Jin was looking for her first job after finishing her degree. She went to a few interviews and noticed an unusual phenomenon: some of the other applicants were bringing a parent with them to the interview. When she asked one of her friends about it, her friend told her, "Hey, that's nothing. The place I work – some parents phone to ask the boss to give their kid a promotion or a raise!" Shocked, Jin asked how that went over with the boss. Her friend raised one eyebrow and asked her, "How do you think?" Jin got the idea and has continued to thank her mom for the lift to her job interviews – but then, wisely, she leaves her in the car (with a window cracked open, of course).

**Still have questions about what to wear?**
If you have read all the stellar advice in this chapter and still have questions about what to wear, try the following:

- Ask the employer what is appropriate.
- Read books like *Managing Your Image Potential* by Catherine Bell.
- Try the quiz opposite. You might not be as clueless as you think.

♥ Chapter 6 ♥

**True or False? Test your dress code savvy \***

| Do you think . . . ? | True | False |
|---|---|---|
| 1. You should always wear a suit to an interview | | |
| 2. It's best to wear black, navy or grey so you'll be taken seriously | | |
| 3. Jeans are okay to wear to an interview as long as the workplace is casual or if you would normally be wearing a uniform | | |
| 4. It's important to avoid wearing perfume or cologne to an interview | | |
| 5. Wear clothes that make you feel comfortable to an interview | | |
| 6. It's okay to borrow clothes to go to an interview | | |
| 7. If you have dyed your hair orange, you should dye it a more "normal" colour before an interview | | |
| 8. What you say is more important than what you wear | | |
| 9. If you're just dropping off an application, you don't have to dress up | | |
| 10. You should never wear white after Labour Day | | |

*Answers on page 107.

# Diving into the Job Dating Pool

On the way to your Dream Job

♥ *Chapter 7* ♥
# One-night stands, transition jobs and other "dating" decisions

So you meet Charming Guy and you know he's not the "forever guy", which would be okay except that you're really looking hard for the "forever guy" but you're temporarily, totally overwhelmed by fascinating and compelling Charming Guy. But oh well, this will be fun at least and so you leap and it IS fun at first but you begin to realize that Charming Guy just doesn't tick all the boxes for you. Maybe it's the annoying way he checks his hair constantly in the mirror when he thinks you aren't looking. Who knows? Bottom line is: Charming isn't cutting it anymore.

This is chemistry – acted upon and then regretted. And despite the pearls of wisdom in this book and the fact that I've been a career counsellor for years, I will admit that I too, have succumbed to chemistry. At least, I'll admit to succumbing to the career kind!

A few years ago, I saw an interesting job on a website I frequent and feeling the pull of something interesting – dare I say "Charming" – I decided to apply. Throughout the application process and interview, I questioned whether this was the right role for me. It had all the hallmarks of Charming Guy. I mean, it looked great – wonderful salary, opportunities for growth, supportive workplace and fascinating colleagues. I was really drawn to it and when I was offered the job, I put the nagging voice inside me on the naughty chair for the afternoon and I accepted the position.

Three days at my new workplace and I knew, with a sinking heart, that it wasn't the job for me. Sure, it was interesting because it was different and I knew that I would learn new things and meet new people but I could already see three to six months down the road when the job would have lost its shiny sparkle. Once the fun new stuff and learning were over, the job itself wasn't the right fit for me. Oops. I had leapt because of chemistry and it led me astray.

Luckily, I managed to get out of the situation with some grace, some sleepless nights and a very red, apologetic face. I managed to extricate myself with the blessing and understanding of my employer. (He didn't even try to sue me for custody of the shiny new nameplate on my office door.) Luckier still, my former employer asked me to come back to my old job. But the headlines just kept rolling through my head:

# ♥ Career Cupid ♥

*"Career counsellor with old résumés stuck to her shoes seen wandering the streets eating a pint of unidentified ice cream".*

I know you won't be shocked to hear me say that after all that, I don't really suggest that leaping on the basis of chemistry alone is a great career strategy. I do, however, recommend Speed Dating, the One-night Stand and Transition Guys.

**Speed Dating**
In Speed Dating, what you're going to do is meet a bunch of new people. Some you will really connect with, while others will simply be an opportunity that won't really go anywhere. Speed Dating sometimes leads to a One-night Stand (we'll talk about that in a bit) and other times...not so much. That's okay though because in all Speed Dating, you have the opportunity to become more visible and also learn more about what's "out there".

In case you haven't guessed by now, Speed Dating is another way of talking about "networking", which is a buzz word I've come to dislike because it sounds so scary and corporate and clichéd. Since networking is, in essence, simply a way for you to meet people and exchange information about work that is mutually interesting, I think of it like Speed Dating. You could also think of it as having coffee for the first time with a bunch of the moms from your kid's soccer team. You sift through a lot of information in a short period of time and see if there's a spark. Then "ding", you're on to the next date.

You know how in dating, people always advise that you "go where the men are"? The same holds true for Career Speed Dating. Let's assume that you want to find out about where the "cool jobs" are, but you have absolutely no connection to those jobs despite having called your Aunt Martha, your sister's manicurist and everyone else in your personal network.

In order to get started, you need to think about where the jobs you are interested in are being done. If you don't have a clue, here's a hint: start with the Yellow Pages of your phone book. It's the most basic directory there is. Let's say you're looking for information about where people who are buyers work. You need a bunch of keywords to help you maximize your search. Even if you don't really know exactly what a buyer does, you can think about what you THINK they do and what draws you to that job in the first place. Maybe, for you, being a buyer is about shopping, being at the mall, having you finger on the pulse of the latest fashion or clothing, scouring department stores and boutiques for the latest retail trends.

For Buyer, your keyword list might look something like this:

# ♥ Chapter 7 ♥

- Shopping
- Merchandising
- Mall
- Clothing
- Purchasing
- Department Store
- Boutique
- Fashion
- Retail

Use these words to look through the Yellow Pages and find organizations that might have Buyers working for them. Then call them to get started on the first step to meeting someone and maybe, setting up a One-night Stand.

Other places to speed date include conferences or meetings for the field you're targeting, professional associations, discussion groups or listservs, and even your local corner store.

Use your favourite search engine and type in Conferences + Buyers + Merchandising (or a couple of your keywords) and see if you can find out where people in your field of interest will be meeting next. Even if you can't afford to attend the conference, it's often relatively easy to volunteer to help with organization beforehand and on the day.

The same goes for finding professional associations. Just as there are mommy groups and book clubs, and Save the Endangered Pencil Sharpener organizations, so too are there associations connected with your field of interest. These associations often have free (my husband's favourite number!) mailing lists that you can get on to sort of "infiltrate" the field. Find out what they're talking about – is it interesting to you? If you're shy or don't speak the language, professional associations' mailing lists are a great place to start Speed Dating. To find associations, try directories at your local library such as:

- *Directory of (American) Associations* (Concept Marketing Group)
- *Associations Canada* (Grey House Publishing)
- *Canadian Key Business Directory* (D&B Canada)
- *Canadian Almanac & Directory* (Micromedia ProQuest)

Often, professional organizations have member lists, allowing you a kind of "one-stop-shop" to find out about more organizations in your

51

♥ *Career Cupid* ♥

field of interest. If you feel intimidated at the thought of phoning "real" employers, try starting with a professional association. Its job is to give information and the people concerned are usually passionate about their subject matter and will love helping a fellow keener learn all about that which is dear to their hearts.

Work up to "Hi, I'm an Aquarius, what's your sign?" when you're ready. Hmmm. Maybe you should read the networking scripts you'll find later in this book instead.

**The One-night Stand**
In career terminology, the One-night Stand is known as "Job Shadowing". I know – it sounds kind of dull or even a bit creepy, which is why I gave it a more exciting label. The Career One-night Stand is every bit as fun and interesting as the romantic One-night Stand, except without most of the risks to your safety and schoolgirl reputation.

The idea is to try on different types of work without having to commit to them. You could interview or even follow around for part of a day, say, a tax lawyer (hey, that's some people's idea of a dream job – don't make fun!) or maybe an architect or a fashion magazine editor. But, I hear you protest, "I don't know any tax lawyers, architects or fashion magazine editors."

That's where Speed Dating comes in so go back to that section if you need some courage. For right now, let's simply talk about what the Career One-night Stand looks like.

- It requires curiosity and a little courage
- It takes very little time
- It involves no long-term commitment
- You can have as many One-night Stands as you have time for
- It allows you to peek in at and "try on" a job that you think might be great
- It lets you thank it for a great time but still leave in the morning with yesterday's clothes on without buying it breakfast

What could be bad about that? Yet, surprisingly few people take the time to enjoy a good One-night Stand here and there. It has occurred to me that perhaps more people would engage in this type of activity if they had the confidence that comes from a bit of a process to follow. Just like its romantic counterpart, the Career One-night Stand can be a spontaneous act stemming from a chance meeting with an attractive target, or it may have some minor planning involved.

♥ Chapter 7 ♥

**For the planners**

1. Think about (or make a list if you are a list-making sort of person) jobs you would like to try.
2. Brainstorm where these jobs will be taking place. Seek help from brainiac friends who always win at things like Jeopardy, if needed.
3. Take a deep breath and using your best "I'm ordering from my favourite catalogue" voice, call the organization and introduce yourself.
4. Ask if there's anyone they would recommend that you speak to in order to find out more about what it's like to work in "Field X". Stress that you are only searching for information about what the career is like, NOT looking for a job.
5. When you reach the appropriate person, SMILE (yes, I know you're talking on the phone, but it really helps make you sound friendly!), then introduce yourself and indicate that you are NOT looking for a job. Tell them that you are considering a career change in the future and are fascinated by the work of "Field X" and you would like to learn more about what it really entails.
6. Let them know that you realize that they are busy and you really appreciate their time. Ask if it would it be possible to make an appointment to speak with them for 10–15 minutes sometime at their convenience so you could ask them some questions about what their day-to-day work involves.
7. Ask them what would be most convenient for them – a face-to-face meeting or one by telephone?
8. If refused, politely ask if there's anyone else they could recommend that you contact.
9. Note down the proposed meeting date, time and details somewhere safe.
10. Reward yourself with something slightly decadent. My suggestions: bubble bath, chocolate milk, screensaver of current Hollywood Heart Throb

This meeting often leads the person you're interviewing to suggest, "Hey, why don't you follow me around for a couple of hours next week to see what I really do?" If they don't suggest it and you feel quite interested in what they do, it may be something you can suggest to them. A couple of hours or half a day walking in your prospective dream job helps you

♥ **Career Cupid** ♥

find out a lot of information very quickly, and with none of the risk of leaping into a new job. This is the groovy thing about the Career One-night Stand.

    You might be wondering why a perfect stranger would be motivated to help you. Here's the "what's in it for them" part: it helps them to develop their sector. In fact, many organizations and people use these opportunities to source out future potential employees, interns, contacts and customers for their field. Your enthusiasm is like candy to them and their sugar buzz might just open doors you hadn't imagined. Once you've had your first One-night Stand, lather, rinse and repeat as often as needed to get some ideas about what looks really fun . . . and what to avoid. Now we move on to (cue the movie trailer guy's booming voice): Transition Guy.

**Transition Guy**
I remember when the first major romance of my young life ended. It had been a tumultuous time full of agony and ecstasy with movie-like airport scenes and a trans-Atlantic love affair that had endured passionately for many years. It was both an immense relief and the worst day of my life when it ended. But out of relationship despair, I was creeping towards feeling that I deserved something equally wonderful in the future – with a happy ending of course! I just wasn't quite ready to try again immediately.

    Once you've dipped your toes in the career dating pool with some Speed Dating and a few One-night Stands, hopefully you'll start to feel motivated to get in a little deeper. I know you're probably scared. I certainly was after my relationship ended. It's the same in career relationships. Even though it might not be right, there may still be lots of truly wonderful parts to it and you may be nervous or sceptical about whether you can find the things it lacks without giving up on the wonderful parts that it has.

    To allay some of your fears and give you some practice, you may want to engage in slightly longer forays into your areas of interest – aka Transition Guy – someone you could spend a bit of time with, but who may not end up being your Happily Ever After place.

    Career Transition Guy includes things like contract work, work exchanges and other forms of temporary work. Whether you're currently working or not, testing out a possible long-term relationship with your dream career is a great way to avoid a divorce down the road.

    If you're working, investigate the possibility of taking a secondment to another, more desirable role within your organization or taking a leave of absence to go outside your organization. Even a few weeks can be helpful! If you're not working or are financially able to leave your

## Chapter 7

current position, consider temporary (maternity or sick leave replacements are opening all the time), contract or project-based work that gets you much closer to your desired field.

Temporary work allows you the chance to try on work you think you will like for a more realistic time frame. It allows you to see some of the "warts" and find out if you can live with them, or if you can do the work slightly differently in the future to get rid of them.

Just like with romantic Transition Guy, you want to be kind and ethical when you enter this type of relationship. Although it might lead to something more permanent, there are no guarantees, so be clear about that. The great thing about contract or other types of short-term work is that it's usually set up with an end date in mind. You are free to discontinue the relationship at that point, without hard feelings. And just like in romance, hopefully at the end of your time with Transition Guy, you're left without a broken heart and more ready to move towards your Happily Ever After at work.

♥ *Chapter 8* ♥
# *Why can't I meet any "nice" jobs?!*

You've got an outfit you feel great wearing. You've checked your teeth and there is definitely no spinach in them. You even managed to find a pair of pantyhose that don't hang down to your knees and whose top doesn't encroach on your newly forming double chin. You've gone where the jobs are and you've introduced yourself to people. You've done a bit of soul-searching and sized up your . . . um . . . assets. You're job dating.

But something doesn't feel right. You're not getting that buzzy, light-headed sensation you expected. Sometimes, your One-night Stands have been less than satisfactory. Speed Dating isn't yielding any promising leads. You're doing everything right but how come all you see are other people who look like they're in career love? Where are all the "nice" jobs for you?!

You know the saying in dating that advises, "Once you stop looking for a great guy, he'll land in your lap"? Well, the same may be true for finding your true love career. Sure, preparation is important. Knowing yourself and thinking specifically about what you're going after are key steps that will help you increase your chances of making a great career match. But I would be misleading you if I didn't admit that there's also some timing and serendipity involved.

**Do you look desperate?**
You know how when you WANT to meet someone, you can't seem to get a second glance, but then as soon as you're off the market, you suddenly appear to be the most desirable woman in the world? That same cosmic mess-with-your-head principle can apply to career dating as well. Somehow, employers and contacts sense the beseeching plea that seems to emanate from your every pore (and you thought it was just the Love's Baby Soft you've worn since you were 12). No matter how calm and composed you think you're being, if your body language is saying, "HELP me . . . I hate my job and I want one like yours", you may find yourself having great meetings with people that never seem to go to a second date. Your desperation is making them feel trapped, nervous and possibly even that you have ulterior motives. Whether it's tantric hot yoga or retail therapy that calms you down, find a way to tap into your

♥ *Career Cupid* ♥

inner Zen . . . or you will end up alone with your Internet favourites permanently stuck on monster.com. And I wouldn't wish that on you. You seem like such a lovely woman.

**Do you scare away your dates?**
The ugly stepsister to appearing too desperate is the woman who scares people. Maybe it's because you come across as too bossy or too high-maintenance but, either way, you're saying to your contacts, "I'm going to be a problem for you or someone you work with".

Sure it's important to be informed and well-presented when you meet with your career "dates", but it's also important to think about what will make your prospective contact feel comfortable. Just as you wouldn't show up to a date with a beer-and-hockey guy wearing a strappy dress and heels, you may want to think about the impression you're giving the contacts you meet. Do you look as if you "fit" the environment in which they work? Do you come across as a "typical but promising" person for the field? Or do you look as if you're too good for the work or gunning for the top job before you've even set foot on the bottom rung?

When you meet people, try to listen more than you talk. Then concentrate on asking questions that are based on what they have just said. This shows you really appreciate their experience and value their advice.

**Will you let them impress you?**
Didn't you learn anything from reading *Seventeen* magazine?! You may have done your research, but just like when you're on a date, you may want to allow the other person to tell you things you already know. Just like in romantic dating, people will enjoy telling you about the great things they've done and help you get to know them. It helps them feel comfortable with you and gives them the sense that they're letting you into their exclusive club. Ask educated questions based on your research, but try to avoid interrogating them.

**How to ask scintillating questions**

- Listen more than you talk
- Ask if it's okay to take notes while you listen
- Make regular eye contact while the person is talking
- Smile and nod to indicate interest in what he or she is saying
- Thank the person profusely while there and then in writing later on

♥ *Chapter 8* ♥

Note how the following questions often start by you revealing some homework you have done to get ready for the conversation. Sorry, I know you thought your homework days were over, but homework is hot, hot, hot!

**Sample questions**

- What does a typical day look like in this job?
- I've read that many people in the field come from a background in _____. What was your journey to this job?
- My research seemed to imply that a major focus of this work is the ability to be good at _____. Would you agree with that?
- Where do you see this field going over the next five to ten years?
- What is your favourite thing about this work? What is your least favourite?

Also avoid telling your "date" everything about themselves or parroting back their website. They already know what they do and what they want is the opportunity to share their take on what they do. The more you can make the meeting like an easy-flowing conversation, the better.

**Looking for love in all the wrong places?**
When things aren't going so well, sometimes it's important to examine where you've been looking. Perhaps it's not what you're saying or doing but where you're looking that's leading you away from career happiness.

Many people find romantic Happily Ever After by meeting a guy in a bar. But that is probably the minority of people. Why? If what you're looking for is long-term commitment, a bar is not as likely to attract the kind of people who are looking for that. Usually, people frequenting bars have a little more immediate goal in mind. I'm not trying to insult people who frequent bars – not at all. It is, of course, possible to meet your dream guy there. But if you've not met him there, it may be time to assess whether there are other, better places to look.

The same goes for career dating. If your dates are turning out to be duds, you may need to rethink your strategy for finding prospects. Just like when you try to expand your romantic search parameters, I suggest that consulting friends and acquaintances about the best places to search for work you will love, is a good plan. After all, 14 heads are better than one.

# ♥ Career Cupid ♥

**Are you sabotaging yourself?**
I have a friend who is probably the most charming person I have ever met. He literally lights up a room when he walks into it and is one of the only people I have ever encountered in real life who exemplifies the word "charisma."

But he has no staying power. He is like a shooting star that dazzles you with all kinds of sparkly light and then quickly dies away before you can catch it in your hand. He is all first impression and has great difficulty with sustained follow through. Or at least, that's what he would have you believe. I have known him a long time and I think he's selling himself short. He has much more to offer than that, but he runs away at the first sign of someone trying to pin down his sparkly tail. He's sabotaging himself. At least, that's what I keep telling him. He insists that he's actually really just that shallow, but I refuse to believe him. What can I say, I'm an optimist!

If you are making a successful initial match but then burning out quickly, try to be honest with yourself. Are you REALLY not making a connection or are you running away when the going gets interesting because it's scary to contemplate a change? Let a few people see your sparkly bits ignite something that will burn longer once in a while and you might find that you have more successful connections than you originally thought.

**If at first you don't succeed . . .**
Yes, the moral of this chapter is that overused cliché. There ARE "nice careers" out there. They aren't always easy to find. You have to believe they exist, you have to get as close to where they are as possible, and you have to periodically assess whether or not it might be you who is messing things up.

Then, get back on that horse, missy!

## ♥ Chapter 9 ♥
# Ready, set . . . his parents!

Yes, you're pretty sure that this job might be "the one". It makes you feel happy inside. You have found yourself doodling your name and new job title in scrolly handwriting in the margins of your books. "Debbie Winthrop, Senior Business Analyst", or "D. Winthrop, Senior Business Analyst", Oh, oh, what about "D.L. Winthrop, Senior Business Analyst"? Like the schoolgirl crush you once had on Derek Cassidy, you're googly-eyed over the prospect of this job. Why else would you put yourself through the torture of control top pantyhose on a sunny Thursday afternoon? Still, you might want to rethink the heart you've used to dot the 'i' in your last name.

But I digress. Congratulations are in order. You've been career dating and you've found work you want to spend some significant time with. You've locked lips with it and found the passion and the future you've been looking for. If this was a romantic relationship, this is the moment when you would be embarking on one of the biggest gigs of the process: meeting his parents. In career dating, this is known as the full-fat, full-foam, ring-a-ding-dong interview. Okay, it's maybe not exactly known as that but I like to call it that. And you really don't want to mess it up.

**Prepare for battle**
As with all meetings, it's good to be prepared. This means that if you have been getting serious about a job, you should anticipate a call asking you to come to "meet his parents". Be prepared so that you don't sound as if it is coming completely out of the blue. Just as you don't want to sound as if you've never heard your boyfriend's parents' names before, you also don't want an employer to think you've forgotten who they are. Keep a file close to your phone or in the electronic device of your choice. Pack it with information about the organization so that you can access it quickly as you're reading. Keep track of any correspondence you've had with the firm because referring to it will let the caller know that you know that you're talking about the same opportunity.

SMILE. You might be scared out of your wits, but you need to sound friendly and competent. People tend not to smile when they're talking

# ♥ Career Cupid ♥

on the phone so make an extra effort to grin, even though you may feel as if you're imitating that smiley Italian chef on the Food Network. Maybe, like her, you'll become rich and well-endowed, too.

Ask questions. He asks you to meet his parents. They call to invite the two of you for dinner. It's natural for you to ask a few questions. What can you bring? Is there a particular wine they prefer? Are there any passive-aggressive tendencies they'd like to get out in the open right now? Okay, maybe not that last one.

When an employer invites you for an interview, ask some questions. Who will you be meeting? What do they do? Would they like to see examples of your work? What's the best way to get to the interview room once you find the building? Should you bring any special equipment (e.g. safety shoes) in case of a tour of the factory? These are all questions that are appropriate to ask. You might want to make a cheat sheet for yourself with your questions on it. I recommend this because sometimes, when an employer calls, you're so excited and/or nervous, you forget what you want to ask. I once forgot to ask, "What time should I be there?" Mind you, that was in Germany and the only words I could remember from German class were useless things like how to say "Fritz, would you like to accompany me to the animal husbandry?" It's a little easier if you're interviewing in your native language. If you're not, don't worry. A little practice and you can even manoeuvre words like "animal husbandry" into the most ordinary of conversations.

**Cheat Sheet**

*Job Title/Role:* Fancy Pants Dream Job

*Organization/Company:* Cool Company

*Estimated length of interview:* 1.5 hours
(meet both interviewers at same time)

*Interviewer(s) name & role:* Ms Pamela Bennett (Director of All Things Important);
Mr Varun Singh (Master of the Universe)

*Location of interview plus directions to specific room:*
123 25th Street, Suite 6A (off expressway, exit 644, turn L at lights, bldg on right). Enter bldg, take elevators to 6th floor. Turn R off elevators and go past washrooms on left. Knock on 2nd last door in hallway (frosted glass)

*Who to ask for upon arrival:* Pamela Bennett

*What to bring:* References (3), extra copy of résumé, work portfolio

♥ Chapter 9 ♥

**Riskier but can be acceptable:**

*Dress code (if you're unsure):* Business casual

*Reimbursement policy for travel expenses* (if you're travelling out of town to attend)

*Types of questions* (Behavioural? Situational? Traditional?)

Stand up. You'll project better, you'll feel better, your stomach will appear flatter. Whether it's staring down the spider in the corner or talking to an employer, standing up will help you feel (and sound) the part of a desirable, skilled commodity. You can scream about the spider after you've hung up the phone.

Practise your small talk. As nervous as you might be when you're faced with the "meet the mother" job interview, it's important to try to sound at least somewhat relaxed. Employers want to know that you are a real person with whom they would like to work. Just as you might compliment your boyfriend's mother's um . . . lovely china bulldog collection, you should try to let the employer know that you think what they are doing looks great. This is the time to harness all the research you've been doing about the field of work, turn on your mega-watt smile and reap the "she's like the daughter I never had" rewards of all your preparation for this very moment. I'm not advocating that you fake enthusiasm. Just like faking other important things in life, it's not going to get you closer to what you want! Hopefully, you actually believe what you're saying because after all, you want to work with them.

**Pick a lipstick that says: I'm someone you will like**
Choose your outfit carefully. Hopefully, you've done enough research on your dream job at this point so that you aren't being forced to compromise your identity for the job. I personally love wearing hats. But you don't want to scare off boyfriend's mother by looking as if he's brought home Pippi Longstocking.

Your aim is to look slightly sparkly and shiny yet familiar. Think of it this way: it's the career equivalent of wearing a pretty sundress to the barbecue dinner where you'll meet boyfriend's parents. It's a little dressier than what you would normally sport for a summer evening dinner, but it still fits the occasion.

The best news? If you like shopping, it's a good excuse to hit the streets in search of something that will make you feel like a million bucks. Read the chapter, "Does This Skirt Make Me Look Fat?" for more tips on what to wear.

## ♥ Career Cupid ♥

**Just what are your intentions young lady?**
In the same way that his father will ask you questions to determine how you came to be standing on his freshly-installed hardwood floors when he didn't know you existed, an employer will ask you some probing questions. Their intention is the same as his father's: to find out if you're really the right person for the job.

So you were shacked up a mere three months ago with another man? Uh huh. And now I'm supposed to believe that you're madly in love with my son? Yep. His father is giving you the evil eye for a reason. He doesn't believe that you really know why you're here. You seem desperate to find a man and get another income to help you pay your condo fees. So what's the deal? Are you just playing with them?

Just as parents feel protective of their sons, employers want to know that you're not just wasting their time by looking for any job. They want to see the look on your face that says you think their job is special. They want to know that you see it for the wonderful opportunity that it is, and that you'll stick around for a while and treat it well, even though it sometimes leaves dirty socks on the floor. Talk specifically about why this work is right for you. Join the dots together so a central, relevant theme runs through your past experiences (and your résumé, cover letter and interview) so it's easy for them to see the purpose and success that have brought you to this incredible opportunity. Just as mothers don't want you to end up with their son by default ("yes ma'am, he was the very last one at the club after all the cute guys had left and I figured smiling at him was better than going home alone to my creepy basement apartment"), employers want to know that you have chosen them. I know, I know. It might seem needy but humour them. While you're humouring them, don't forget to be enthusiastic and sincere.

**Objects in mirror are closer than they appear**
Now comes the hot seat. They're staring at you, pens poised. It feels as if they're barrelling down on you at 60 mph. It's time for you to answer some questions. The object of this exercise is simple: are you really who you say you are? Do you have what we are looking for? Do we feel comfortable with you?

Don't worry. This isn't about being perfect. It is about being genuine, specific and likeable. If you're too vague, what you're really saying is, "Trust me, you'll like me" – but without any proof, they're not buying it.

Tell true stories from your life and work. Show how you think about things and what you do when faced with challenges. Think of and talk about specific examples that help the employer get to know you and

♥ Chapter 9 ♥

your work style better. Be very, very concrete, e.g. "Last Thursday, I spent the day collating stats for our annual report and this is what happened…". While it's definitely a bad idea to rehearse answers (mothers and employers have amazing antennae that pick up on that kind of thing), it is a great idea to prepare a little. Like mothers, employers have many standard questions that you'll start to recognize over time. If you haven't even thought about them before the meeting, you might be doomed from the start.

**Helpful Hints**

| Parents' questions | Employer's questions |
|---|---|
| Why do you love our son? | Why do you want this job? |
| Do you know that he leaves the toothpaste cap off? Why do you still love him? | What looks like the most frustrating thing about this job? What looks most interesting? |
| Tell us what cute stories he's told you from his past. We're sure he left the really good stuff out. Do you still love him even though he's done these embarrassing things? | How did you find out about us? What do you know about us? |
| How will you help our son reach the potential we know he has? | What can you do for us? |
| Will you stay for the long haul or will you run at the first sign of snoring like his last girlfriend? | Where do you see yourself in five years? |

**Going in for the kill**
Everything is going reasonably well and all of sudden his mother looks at you, all innocence and mascara over her teacup and says, "So, Eric tells me that you have six tattoos. How interesting!"

This is the part of the meeting where you get the fun job of talking about your weaknesses. It's important to remember that weaknesses are in the eye of the beholder (in this case, the mother or employer) and have little to do with what you perceive your own weaknesses to be. You might not think that your six tattoos are a problem but if she does, then

65

# ♥ Career Cupid ♥

it's your job to talk about them in a positive way and help her see that they are not reasons to disqualify you from loving the man (or job) of your dreams.

In an employment interview, scrutinize your résumé and yourself carefully. Are there any obvious cracks in your presentation? Do you have gaps in employment or a scattered career history or a lack of experience or really frizzy hair? Prepare to acknowledge and talk specifically about what you've learned from your mistakes. If you're asked to pick a weakness, choose something that is real but not overwhelmingly scary to the employer. Let's face it. While frizzy hair is tragic, it's not a life-or-death issue so it may be wise to pick something fairly benign such as this when you're asked. (Note to reader: the frizzy hair is merely cited as an amusing example. I don't advise using it in an employment interview.) Whatever the weakness, move on quickly to the strategies you're using to improve (e.g. "I wanted to take some responsibility for my frizzy hair so I went out and found some really great moisturizing shampoo at Wal-Mart last week. After using it for a few days, I've already noticed an improvement"). If you are the proud owner of naturally glossy, frizz-free coiffure but you lack relevant work experience then perhaps your weakness might sound a little more like, "As someone transitioning into a career in purple shoe design, I have been seeking ways to gain more industry experience and I was fortunate to be able to build my design skills by volunteering at an orange shoe-making factory. While the shoe colour is naturally different from what your organization does, this opportunity provided me with hands-on experience in the shoe manufacturing process, which will be helpful to you if I am offered the role of purple shoe designer."

Being authentic but positive and focusing on your strategies allows the employer to see that you want to improve and that you can take concrete action. This will allow them to remember these positive qualities, rather than focus on your weaknesses.

**Mmmm . . . this meatloaf is delicious**
Don't be tempted to lie. If you really think the meatloaf is delicious, say so. If you are choking it down and wondering about the significance of the "decorative" swirl of ketchup on the top, don't lie and say you love it. When you fib in the interview, it tells the employer (and boyfriend's mother) that you can't be trusted on the job. It also means that you may be talking yourself into a position that isn't right for you. Maybe you can handle a little dried-out meatloaf with ketchup swirl every once in a while. Every job has some of that. But if you're going to be eating that every day and you hate it, maybe this isn't the right job for you. You're trying to find Happily Ever After at work, remember? This is not the time

## Chapter 9

for deluding yourself. Remember that you are on a quest for something magical and the truth will set you free! Well, possibly after a short period of imprisonment during which you lose all hope but as in all truly magical quests, eventually this dark period will go away and the happy ending will reveal itself. Disney and I practically guarantee it!

♥ **Chapter 10** ♥

# Proposals, prenuptials and job offers

There you are in front of thousands at Marine World and Dolly the Dolphin swims up to you with a sparkly ring nestled snugly on a life jacket. Congratulations! The employer proposed! You're ready to take the plunge and settle down with a great job. Maybe it's your dream job. Okay, maybe it's your dream job *for now* (that ring is really sparkly and all the chlorine in the air is making your head spin a little). I know you feel giddy and convinced that you've found "the one" and nothing will ever come between you. Whatever your state of euphoria or chlorine intake, it's important in this day and age to consider a little thing all the folks in Hollywood (and executive washrooms) know well. It's called "the Prenup".

**To thine own self be true**
Before your start gushing "yes" in front of thousands of Marine World viewers, it's important to consider the proposal. Try to avoid focusing on the sparkly ring for a second. Yeah, that means you. Yoo hoo! I'm over here.

While you've been gaga at the sparkly, your employer has been waiting for an answer. And frankly, they're a little insulted that you haven't leaped right in there and said yes. It's important at this moment to make them feel that their efforts haven't been wasted and that their hopes won't go unfulfilled. But you must do this without committing to anything yet. You may wish to compliment them on the quality of the ring and how flattered you are to be offered it. You could add something that tells them that you're seriously considering their proposal and would like to respond to them as quickly as possible. You might suggest a private meeting where you could give them a proper answer and talk to them about your future plans. All these actions assist the employer to know that you are seriously interested in their proposal . . . but they don't lead you down the road towards an exit reminiscent of Julia Robert's *Runaway Bride*.

It's important that you're not committed yet, because before you get caught up in a Sally Field moment of "They love me, they really love me", you need to think about whether you really love them. Does this

♥ *Career Cupid* ♥

job tick many of the boxes on your wish list? Are the boxes it doesn't tick able to be worked towards in some other way or at a later date? Have you spent enough time with this job to be fairly certain that you'll still love it in the times when all your girlfriends are going out for date nights and you're spending the night at home snuggled up on the couch with your same old career?

Don't misunderstand me. No career is perfect. But you want to have enough hope and passion and love for it at the beginning to sustain you through some of the inevitable bumps in the road. If it's not your dream job, does it sustain you in some practical way that will help you move closer to your dream (or pay off your looming Visa bill?) If not, consider rejecting the offer. But leave the door open for future opportunities. Just because this isn't the right opportunity for you now, doesn't mean that it won't be in the future. There is also the possibility that you will meet or work with this employer in another job you decide to accept. As Star Wars' Yoda would say, "skilled is the woman who can gently break a Jedi's heart". Oh wait, that was just me doing my goofy imitation of a Muppet.

**Marriage or cohabitation?**
Many people decide to postpone (or swap) the commitment of marriage for the option of living together. If you have dated your possible career, engaged in some One-night Stands and you still aren't positive that this is the career for you, try doing some contract work to start. Depending on how great your fear of commitment is, you could go for longer contracts or even a so-called "permanent job" as long as you know you can stay for at least a year or two. If you're still feeling uncertain about the work, it's in your best interests to opt for short-term project contracts, register with temporary employment agencies, seek maternity leaves or sick leaves so that you are able to vacate the position after a relatively short period of employment and still fulfill your commitment. This keeps your employer feeling favourably towards you because you have held up your end of the bargain. And that can spell "fabuloso reference", not to mention opportunities to be considered for longer-term or more interesting positions.

But remember that even in romantic relationships, some laws state that cohabitating couples hold the responsibilities of a legally married couple after a certain length of time. Unless both you and your employer have agreed to it, be careful that you don't start giving and receiving the message that your temporary job is a long-term commitment. That only leads to hurt feelings, broken promises and all the other juicy things that we were promised in our last "best buy for the beach" novel.

♥ Chapter 10 ♥

### Yes! (I do, I do, I do)

The sparkly is aiming for your finger and the next question you need to ask yourself is, "how does it fit?" Rather than spending the next umpteen years with a ring that is too tight or too loose, now is the time to make the necessary adjustments so that it fits you perfectly. This is the time for negotiating the terms of your agreement with the employer. In case you have missed the "enough already" metaphor of this book, there are again, striking similarities between romance and career relationships.

### Helpful Hints

| *Accepting a proposal of marriage* | *Accepting a job* |
|---|---|
| Agree on a wedding date | Agree on a start date |
| Arrange the honeymoon | Find out about probationary period |
| Negotiate where you'll set up house | Find out about your work space |
| Create or update wills and powers of attorney | Find out about health plans and benefits |
| Start dreaming about and saving for your second honeymoon | Discuss vacation benefits |
| Let him know you're thrilled to be marrying him | Let employer know that you're thrilled to be working with the organization |

Remember that your employer, like your betrothed, has probably spent considerable time and thought crafting an agreement for you to consider. Be gentle but firm with your suggestions for adjustment to the original agreement. Ask questions so that you can determine whether you're interpreting their terms correctly. Frame your questions in an open-ended manner to promote discussion, rather than making the employer feel defensive. "Can you tell me more about the rationale

# ♥ Career Cupid ♥

behind the salary?" may be received better than, "Why is the pay so low?" Like every discussion in a relationship, it is your duty to negotiate gracefully and realistically the terms of your agreement so that in the end, you both feel comfortable – even if you didn't get absolutely everything you wanted. Now is the not the time to be a doormat or a dominatrix. Find a happy middle ground and then . . . you guessed it . . . be happy about it!

## Thou art officially old
If the work you are entering comes with the possibility of a pension plan, you want to find out the details. Many organizations will have a book they can give you that outlines how the plan works and whether you can take your money out of it down the road and transfer it to another plan of your choosing. Just as it might feel ugly to ask your guy about retirement (hate to conjure up images in his head about you looking 80), it's still important information to consider.

Yes, you will probably feel "officially old" when pension plans become important to you. But, I for one know I'll still love the cheese capelletti at my favourite Italian eatery when I'm 70ish. Having a pension plan as one option to pay for it is good news indeed. If one isn't available when you negotiate your work agreement, consider other savings options for your future. A girl's gotta eat!

## The Prenup
Some employers will be very formal and want you to sign a contract when you accept a job. Like several well-known Hollywood starlets who succumbed to the charms of a handsome bodyguard and lived to regret it, the employer may simply want to be clear about where things stand from the start. It's not that they don't love you or are unromantic. They are just realistic. You, like many Hollywood bodyguards, may in turn wish to have a lawyer or trusted friend waiting in the wings to review the contract. It's not that you don't love them or are unromantic. You are just realistic as well.

This process might feel cold and calculating to you. It might even cause you to question your true feelings for the work or their true feelings for you. It is, however, not uncommon for all parties to work out explicitly what they are agreeing to do. Ask questions. Negotiate as needed. Then, as long as you are not signing away your legal rights or your soul, and you can live with the terms of the agreement, it's quite a common part of modern upscale marriages – and careers.

For those among you who have never been faced with a career prenup, lucky you. Romance is not dead! But remember that the law still protects both you and the employer anyway. Accepting even the

# Chapter 10

most romantic of proposals comes with legal stuff attached to it, whether you sign anything or not. I know – it makes a girl feel kinda cheap and dirty, doesn't it?

# Landing Your Dream Job

## And living Happily Ever After at Work

♥ Chapter 11 ♥

# When good women go baggy

I was in the hairdresser's one Saturday about 15 years ago getting my semi-annual highlights when I witnessed something that shook the modern sensibilities I fancied myself possessing. On the other side of the mirror from me sat a woman who was of an age where she probably came to the hairdresser each week for something I've heard my grandmother call a "wash and set". I grew up with one girly grandmother who was the "wash-and-set" sort while my other inventive grandmother was much more of a do-it-yourselfer. Inventive grandma was always fascinated by contraptions so while she didn't go for this mysterious weekly appointment called the "wash and set", she did have a hilarious circa 1960 vacuum-cleaner hairdryer. It had, in its day, apparently been touted as the next great thing. I'm not sure who thought that teaming a Filter Queen and a hairdryer was a good idea but it sure made for some funny evenings trying to dry our hair after swimming in the lake.

    Anyway, the woman in the hairdressing shop that day appeared to be a kindred spirit to my girly grandmother. She sat in her chair in her stylish shoes and matching handbag, chatting pleasantly with her hairdresser. She appeared quite relaxed and jovial as her hair was transformed into a mass of little pink curlers. All of a sudden, her hairdresser uttered what were apparently loud and terrifying words: "Lucy, your husband's coming!"

    I have never seen a 75-year old woman move so quickly in my life. She was out of that chair in a flash with her pink curlers clattering and bobbing in the wind. She got about two feet across the floor but then stood paralyzed in the middle of the salon with her cape flapping, looking frantically around for a place to hide. Suddenly inspired, the salon receptionist yelled, "In here Lucy!" and beckoned to the woman to step into the broom-closet-sized vestibule where the stylists mixed their potions and lotions. Lucy darted in quickly and the receptionist slammed the door. There was a deafening silence as everyone paused, transfixed, just as the husband reached the door to the salon and entered. Scissors flashed and stilted conversations quickly resumed in an effort to mask the drama that had just unfolded.

# ♥ Career Cupid ♥

"May we help you?" Lucy's hairdresser stepped forward like a warrior approaching the enemy. It turned out that Lucy's husband Bruce was half-way to the hardware store before realizing that Lucy had forgotten her checkbook in the car. Eyes downcast, he handed it over to the hairdresser as if it was an unexploded bomb and ducked quickly out of the salon as fast as he had appeared.

Once the all-clear was sounded, Lucy appeared from her hidey-hole looking slightly flushed but relieved. "Goodness, that was close!" she said, "In 48 years of marriage, he's never seen me without full hair and makeup before!"

My 20-year-old self was astounded. I couldn't imagine having a lifelong relationship with my husband without him once seeing me with bed head or finding a tampon box in the bathroom trash. I mean, did this Lucy woman get up at 4:00 in the morning to prepare for her husband's awakening? I snorted and thought, "As if!"

Now that I'm a little older, I can see that some of the mystery that Lucy and Bruce held in their relationship might be appealing. Don't get me wrong, I would never forgo the um . . . intimacy . . . yeah, that's the right word, that comes with revealing your unprimped self to your loved one but perhaps I have more appreciation than I did back then for the way Lucy and Bruce arranged things.

We are, in general, much more casual in our relationships than we were a few decades (heck, even a few years) ago. And while I am a big promoter of authenticity at work, I also believe in professionalism. Everyone has their own definition and parameters for professionalism so drawing the lines around this topic isn't an exact science. However, I have noticed that in some cases, during a long career relationship, some good women can go baggy.

**You don't bring me flowers anymore**
You used to be the one coming up with the great ideas. You contributed in meetings, you wrote proposals, you innovated products or practices in ways that made the employer and you look good. But just like the Neil Diamond/Barbara Streisand song goes, "You don't bring me flowers anymore", perhaps you have become bored or uninspired with your work. Maybe you're overtired with other life obligations and you just don't have the energy for career romance anymore. Whatever the reason, you have started resting comfortably in a place where you feel that you don't really need to be the star – after all, why not let the up-and-comers dazzle with their flash?

Just like in romance, you will settle into a less intense phase of your work after the initial heady days of courting and honeymoon are over. The trick is to find the balance before you end up looking as if you don't

## Chapter 11

care enough to put any effort in at all anymore. While you're probably not staying up late six nights a week coming up with your next amazing idea, it's important not to give up innovating altogether. Every career needs a little romantic gesture thrown in on a regular basis.

**Ways to keep the career romance alive**

- Collaborate with other people on projects – because you're sharing the load, you often get to choose the bits that you find most fun and are skilled at. People may even call you "sparkly" in an awed sort of voice!

- Take time off – sometimes we forget to give ourselves permission to take holiday time or even short unpaid leaves to recharge. You're fabulous but you're not irreplaceable and being away for a while may allow you to return with fresh enthusiasm. Just remember to clean your stuff out of the lunchroom fridge before you go . . . it will look scary by the time you get back.

- Get some rest – it can be difficult with all that you have going on but maybe you need to scale back a bit in some areas so that work can be approached with energy. P.S. Energy doesn't come from a mug, can, bottle or the vending machine. Hint: exercise and more sleep will help you figure out two of the main places energy comes from!

- Recommit to the work – sometimes work slides down our priority list when other things keep us busy. Revisit your priorities and shuffle things if needed. Approach work with the same enthusiasm as a second honeymoon.

Don't force your employer to sing, 'You don't bring me flowers'. It makes you look bad and will probably be painful to your ears. They are, after all, mostly tone deaf despite playing "background singer no. 2" in the community theatre production of *Mamma Mia*.

**Don't you want a girlfriend who's hot like me . . .**
The giddy, heady days of your new job are gone and you've settled into a comfortable routine. Your tendency these days is to open your closet and throw on the nearest thing that's reasonably clean and head out the door for work. But ask yourself honestly: have you let yourself go? If you spend all your time at home wearing flannel pyjamas with Dorito dust sprinkled down the front of them, you're essentially saying to your man, "I've got you and now I don't have to put any more effort in." Granted, he's probably not dazzling you with his uniform of grungy baseball cap

## ♥ Career Cupid ♥

and hockey jersey either, but if you put a little effort in on a regular basis, you might be pleasantly surprised at the results. By results, I mean that you'll feel better (some of us women still haven't learned that you can't change someone else). Who feels attractive and worthy of their life when they're sporting last week's snacks down their front? Just like in romantic marriage, sometimes, things can slide a little too far towards the category of "I just don't care anymore".

If you're feeling as if your workplace isn't treating you the same way they did during the giddy days of first career love, think about whether you're holding up your end of the bargain. While you don't have to look as if you're dressed to go to an interview every day, it is important to check the mirror before you head off to work. Does the image you see reflecting back at you look like someone who engenders a feeling of competence in a stranger/client/boss? If not, you should rethink your look. After all, if you hear your employer humming "Don't you want a girlfriend who's hot like me . . . ", they may be dreaming about finding someone who can represent them in something better than your customary "but they're so comfortable and cheap!" cargo pants.

### Who—o-o-o-o are you?

You started doing this work when you were fresh out of school or just had your first baby. You're now a woman with years of valuable experience in her Victoria's Secret Miracle bra. Chances are you're not the same person you were when you started working oh those many years ago. But is your wealth of life and career experience reflected in your day-to-day work? Are you still treated or viewed in the same way you were way back when? You may be doing the same work you were then, but you're not the same person. You have valuable skills and experience to offer. It's time to reinvent yourself a little.

Seek out opportunities to try new things, whether at work or outside of working hours. Don't be afraid to take on new responsibilities or look at your job and see if you can take it in slightly new directions. Investigate opportunities to move into secondment or acting positions where you can stretch yourself and revitalize your energy. Volunteer for something that is completely new for you. Think about the theme song to the crime drama *CSI*. Who—o-o-o-o are you? Who do you want to show yourself to be? Maybe it's not the same person you were in 2006. Keep reinventing yourself.

### Raspberry beret

When I was thinking about a song to represent this section, for some reason I thought of the song, "Raspberry Beret". I'm not sure why because I don't really know the words. Perhaps it is because I think that

# ♥ Chapter 11 ♥

a raspberry beret sounds fun and festive and like something a hat-loving woman like me would want to aspire to. You can talk amongst yourselves about whatever analogy works best for you.

Many women talk about work they would like to do in the future. But they sabotage themselves by looking and acting exactly like someone who is doing their current job. Your goal is to look as if you fit your current work but have people thinking, "Wow, she would be even better in that job over there. This one is really not maximizing her talents."

What I'm trying to say is that it's important to think and dress and behave aspirationally. Look to the future and your goals. Cultivate a mentor relationship with someone you admire in the field by staying in regular contact (at their convenience) and learning from their advice. Start building a network in the field for which you are headed. Along the way, think, dress and behave in ways that will lead you towards those distant hills. I'm not suggesting that you adopt an arrogant "this job is beneath me" attitude, but thinking about where you would like to be on your next career step is important. Proactively engaging in activities and behaviours that are normal for people in those positions is a good strategy. It will help people see you as someone fit for where you're going, not simply where you are. That's your raspberry beret. Yummy!

**Lucy, you got some 'splaining to do!**
Back to Lucy and her 48 years of keeping her husband in the dark about what she really looked like. Bruce presumably married Lucy under the impression that her hair looked a certain way and had a certain colour. He might use the famous line, "Lucy, you got some 'splaining to do!" if he found out what she really looked like. While I admittedly find this marital agreement somewhat offensive and certainly labour-intensive, I also think that it might be a good model to use for career relationships.

No matter how comfortable you feel at work or how long you've worked there, it's important to keep some of your hair and makeup under wraps. Baring all in these days of reality TV and tabloids seems like the norm but the rules of Hollywood usually don't apply in real life. Instead, try for authentic professionalism. Be yourself (let's face it, it's too tiring to be anyone else what with all the other stuff you've got going on) but be the professional version of yourself. Letting it all hang out at work can be tempting but it's dangerous. Think about how you'd feel if your Christmas party antics were caught on tape and shown at the next staff meeting. People remember stuff like that for a long, long time and you might find that you're wishing you could hide in the closet with your pink curlers, just like Lucy.

# ♥ Chapter 12 ♥
# Your cheatin' heart

If you eagerly turned to this chapter when you read the table of contents, I am guessing that you're either in a hot and heavy affair right now or you're possibly contemplating getting into a hot and heavy affair. As Hugh Grant says, "You saucy minx!"

It's estimated that more than 40 percent of married women will have an affair at some time over the course of their marriage. This is despite the whole cohabitation, then often extravagant "do you, do you" ceremonies that many couples go through to get into the married state in the first place.

In the workplace, there's none of that "what colours are your girls wearing" extravaganza when you sign on the dotted line for a job. We don't fork out thousands and thousands of dollars for the big day, nor do we have to solemnly swear in front of anybody that we'll commit to staying at Flap Jack Attack for the rest of our lives. Even signing what looks like a formal contract isn't enough to scare many people into staying in a job they hate. So I'm thinking that if cheating is reaching epic proportions in marriages, it's got to be running rampant through workplaces.

### Cheating at the altar

A couple of years ago I was at a wedding. Late in the evening, I was startled to see the bride in a seriously compromising position. What a startling juxtaposition to observe her in her wedding dress playing hot and heavy tonsil tennis with a guy who was not the groom!

Many people commit this same act of cheating in their career, especially in the peak of job-search frenzy. They accept a job but then immediately continue going after something they think is better, completely disregarding the commitment they have already made to the first job. I think the reasons for this type of cheating are many. Fear is probably up there as a factor. Then there's greed, apathy, uncertainty and some of the other seven dwarves.

Cheating at the altar can happen easily because sometimes we are so desperate to get a job – any job – that we leap at the first offer, without really thinking about it. We just want to have *something*. But we can't

♥ *Career Cupid* ♥

commit because we know instinctively and usually fairly immediately by the sinking in our stomachs, that it's not the right job for us. It's much harder to stay with that icky job for the recommended year or turn it down in the first place to wait – with no guarantees – for the right job to come along.

The reality is that sometimes you'll have to take the icky job. You need it to put a roof over your head and you need it NOW. Ideally, if you're in this situation, you should search for jobs that are inherently short-term by nature. This might include registering with temporary employment agencies or taking small contracts that will tide you over while you do your longer-term job search. If you contribute productively and enthusiastically (despite your general boredom with the work), this strategy may allow you the possibility of gaining a positive reference from your immediate employer that you can use towards your longer-term opportunities. It will also avoid the common situation where employers in the same field "tattle" on employees who renege on their offers. Due to the time, expense and effort organizations go through in order to recruit one person, you may find that you end up on a sort of black list in your field if you cheat an employer (or give them the impression that you were using them to get a negotiating position with another organization). They can be quite efficient at spreading your name and story around when they're particularly unhappy and short on their coffee drinks du jour.

**Emotional affairs**
You're not actually cheating . . . yet, but you've lost that loving feeling at work. Your body is at work but your soul and mind are off riding horses with a guy who looks remarkably like Brad Pitt. In this case, the guy who looks remarkably like Brad Pitt is "that job over there that looks so much cooler/better/easier than mine". You're having an emotional affair with the job down the hall. Oh sure, you haven't slept with it yet, but it looks awfully cute and you're spending all your free time lusting after it and text messaging about it and planning what you'd do if you got it. You're ignoring your current job, which suddenly looks full of flaws and incredibly demanding to boot. The way the photocopier jammed up on you on Fridays used to be cute but now it's just plain irritating. Job down the hall's photocopier never jams.

While you're not guilty of outright cheating, you are having an emotional affair. Your heart has turned a corner away from your current job, leaving it swinging in the wind, wondering what it did wrong. The question is, are you having an incredibly cow-like "the grass is always greener" episode, which would be cured by a good

# ♥ Chapter 12 ♥

old-fashioned Career One-night Stand or is this something more serious?

Try the Career One-night Stand as a level one cure. See if the job really is as great as you dreamed. You might find that looking from over there down the hall back at your job, you suddenly remember why it seemed so cute when you took it all those eons ago.

If, after your One-night Stand, you still find your heart skips a beat every time you think about the other job, you may need to take more serious action. Yes, I'm talking about engaging in some career dating. It's not just for the young and nubile, you know. Sure, the rules may have changed since you were "out there" way back when, but that's what this book is for! Who knows, you might even find you like it and want to play the field for a while.

**Cheating when the love is gone**
You know it. Your employer should know it if they care about you at all. You've tried to fix things but they just aren't putting in the same effort as you are. They don't talk to you anymore or seem interested in anything you're doing. You still love them as a *friend* but you don't feel the passion anymore. You're on the rocks and heading towards divorce.

So what's wrong with a little cheating? So you're sneaking out early and spending hours at work surfing the Internet or working on personal stuff. Everyone knows the relationship is over. It's just a matter of having the conversation. Who's really getting hurt in this situation?

The answer to that question is you. Just like having a romantic affair when you're in a committed relationship, you are risking discovery and a relationship that will not only end, but will probably end with a messy finale. That guilt you feel but then justify is your conscience's way of telling you that what you're doing is wrong, wrong, wrong. You know it is but you're in a state where you are ignoring it because you're desperate for something – happiness at work. So you find it where you can and in doing so, you cheat your employer (and yourself) along the way.

If you're cheating in this way (and I think a lot of people are without actually admitting it to themselves), you owe it to yourself to be a bit patient. I know it's difficult but sometimes getting out of a less-than-ideal situation takes a bit of time. Think of this as "preserving your reference letters and ability to move to a great new job without your current employer exacting revenge for your cheating" time. Use good judgment to go after your career happiness in a forthright, ethical way. If you think there's hope, read the ideas in the chapter called, *When Good Women*

# ♥ Career Cupid ♥

*Go Baggy*. If you have given up on the relationship, read the chapter on divorce. Whatever your situation, you need to take action! Don't wait another minute to start working towards getting your groove back because sneaking around cheating isn't the way to help you stand tall in your kicky new boots. They are fab. They deserve the limelight. And so do you.

**Cheating isn't really cheating when it's true love**
It would feel wrong if it weren't so right. The job of your dreams has finally appeared! You want it but you can't quite leave your current job yet. Maybe there's a contract to consider or a project to finish or some medical bills that only this job's insurance will cover. Whatever the reason for staying, this is the kind of cheating that is so wonderful, so fabulous that it won't even feel like cheating. You'll be so wrapped up in your own happiness at having found what you think is "the one", that you'll be convinced that cheating is the right thing to do.

What does cheating look like in this case? It can take many forms. In some cases it's squeezing out your current work responsibilities to start taking on projects in your new dream job. At other times, it's simply mentally checking out of your current job by planning and dreaming about the one on the horizon.

This is the career equivalent of keeping your current romantic relationship going while you actively work on a new one and see if dream guy will work out. It can be really tempting to approach transition this way. After all, being alone or not having a backup plan is plain scary and often financially impractical.

It's fine to go after your dream job, of course! It's also natural to want to ensure that you have your ducks in a row before you make the leap. The key is to be ethical and fair to the one you are dumping. As in romance, treat the dumpee as you would want to be treated if you were being dumped and not the way that Jimmy Whatshisname treated you when he left you for your best friend in grade 11. Don't use work time to investigate other work or go to interviews. Avoid searching for or sending job applications from your work computer and email address. Engaging in these types of activities is the career equivalent to sleeping with someone else in your partner's bed. This is no misdemeanour we're talking about here. This has serious, painful and career-derailing consequences. Everyone does it, you say? Well, if "everyone" jumped off a bridge, young lady, would you? Unlike romantic relationships, your next employer WILL ask your "ex" for a reference. How many times has your prospective boyfriend asked to speak with your last one before he would date you? Are you feeling the danger of cheating yet?

♥ **Chapter 12** ♥

**Aim for manageable torment**

*Top reasons people quit their jobs*

- Inadequate compensation
- Inadequate opportunities for career advancement
- Insufficient recognition or appreciation
- Boredom
- Inadequate benefits
- Inadequate opportunities for professional development
- Insufficient job security
- Undesirable impact on health or stress level
- Poor relations with management
- Undesirable commute

*(Source: Dan Malchowski, Salary.com)*

I'm not suggesting that there is a "stay until you die" mandate when you take a job. The reality is that many workers today will have a minimum of 8–12 different jobs within their career. Career counsellors like me have been throwing around stats like that for years. Perhaps the fault lies partially with us then, since we're giving the impression that people move around frequently in their working lives. Sometimes that movement is of the worker's own choosing and other times workers are forced to make a change because of circumstances thrust upon them. With many companies down-sizing and hiring on short-term or contract bases instead of offering so-called "permanent" jobs, it's not a stretch to think that some people feel minimal loyalty to their employer. Not every situation is ideal and sometimes you'll find yourself in a cheating situation where you'll actually feel justified. But just like in romantic relationships, patience and judgment play a big role in how successfully you navigate the bumps. Ask yourself if your judgment has become a little skewed. Sometimes waiting out a less than stimulating situation for a while is the prudent course. I think that HOW you treat people while you're in the relationship is also very important. Managing to leave an unsuccessful one gracefully is a key to your long-term ability to look at yourself in the mirror and torment yourself merely about your "my hairdresser obviously decided she hates me" hairstyle instead of your guilty conscience.

## ♥ Chapter 13 ♥
# Sex isn't everything but . . .

Just like in romantic relationships, in the old days, people didn't tend to get divorced. Instead, they usually opted to get into a serious career relationship when they were quite young and then they stayed there until retirement or death (and, let's face it, even the most youth-obsessed people among us usually want to reach the bocce ball and Velcro shoes phase, rather than face keeling over the filing cabinet at work).

Today, things are quite different. As I mentioned in the last chapter, there can be considerable job change and movement during a career. For many, that movement will feel not nearly frequent or fast enough. For others, it will strike terror into their hearts at the thought of moving around so much. The facts remain that whether you choose to divorce a job or it divorces you, you will have to deal with inevitable change during your career.

### When his breathing annoys you
How do you know when it's time for you to divorce your job? To use the relationship metaphor again, it's obvious you need to at least consider leaving when very basic things start to grate on you. Just as it's not reasonable for you to expect that your man will stop breathing because you think he's doing it too loudly, it's not reasonable for you to expect that your employer will change the fundamental way that they do things. If you have tried to work within the system, tried to change it and tried to change yourself but still frequently find yourself crying in the last stall of the women's washroom on the fifth floor, it may be time for you to consider leaving your job. Ask yourself, as you dry your eyes, how far down the road to going Baggy you really are. After all, you're a great girl and it would be pity for you to send an over-the-top, hysterical, name-calling nasty-gram through the company email just because someone happened to leave their dirty coffee mug in the office sink again.

### When you've heard the same stories a hundred times
You know how when you've been with someone a while, you start to know by heart the humorous anecdotes that they trot out at every cocktail party and family gathering? The same goes for work. When you find yourself zoning out after the first two syllables in meetings because

# ♥ Career Cupid ♥

"you've heard it all before", you may be suffering from a repetitive strain injury of the listening kind. You have lost your faith that anything new and interesting can happen in this relationship and thus, you may be creating a self-fulfilling prophecy.

### When the sex has become predictable
Bonuses, raises, new responsibilities – all these things used to excite you. But lately, they've become staid and predictable. You know exactly what's going to happen and when. It's the same routine – year in and year out – and what used to make your pupils dilate and your breathing get a little faster, now just feels...dull. You've lost the spark you used to feel when you came to work. If you can't generate some heat soon, it's time to think about leaving. Just like in a relationship, the sex isn't everything but when it's not working, everything else is affected and electronics will only take you so far. I'm talking about the new combination phone/webmail/dvd playing/coffee machine you got from the boss – what were you thinking?

### When your fantasies start taking over
There you are at the company picnic or a conference and you find yourself lusting after another job. I'm not just talking about glancing appreciatively at the other options. You realize that you're thinking how much you seriously DESPISE that woman who has the really interesting job with company X. You have to bite your lip the whole time to keep from launching yourself in a breathless, frantic rush at the rep from Company Y. You find yourself daydreaming at your desk/cash register/computer more than you're actually working. This is a sign that you're already well on your way down the cheating road (in fact you've already passed a few exits).

### When he hardly seems to notice you
Just like in a romantic relationship, there may be signs in your job that a divorce is imminent. One of the first clues may be a lack of attention. Where you used to be consulted and asked for advice, now your opinions and ideas never seem to go anywhere. Kathy Bates' character in Fried Green Tomatoes tried to get her husband to notice her by greeting him at the door dressed only in cellophane. If you find that your (work appropriate) grand gestures and attempts to contribute are being overlooked, it may be a clue that you're on your way out. P.S. No matter what the question, cellophane, in the manner of Kathy Bates is usually not the answer. It's like putting a magnifying glass on all your wrinkly bits!

♥ Chapter 13 ♥

**When he accuses you of things**
Sometimes, when a man is getting ready to suggest a break-up, it can feel as if he's on the attack. Every little thing you do is wrong, wrong, wrong. The same occurs at work. Being brought up for discussion or treating yourself or your colleagues badly may be a symptom of your unhappiness. These are signs that either you need to change how you are doing things or get ready for a career divorce. Even in this less-than-pleasant circumstance, some career relationships can be saved. Maybe you can change, learn a new skill or adapt to the new regime. Often the employer is willing to work on things with you. This is a good sign. But still a sign that the word "divorce" has been uttered somewhere along the line, so take it seriously.

**When he seems more interested in someone else**
You used to be the zip in his zippity-doo-da. Now, you seem to be the anchor weighing him down. Suddenly, he perks up when someone else is around and you have become something like the fake wood panelling on your basement walls – dated, bland and at serious risk of being replaced. Although every workplace has its cycles and rhythms, if your rising star has suddenly stalled, it may be that you need to assess your options. See if you are staying current with the needs of the organization…or you risk it moving on to someone who looks and performs less like varnished pressboard.

**For the sake of the children**
Whether you find yourself being divorced or you do the divorcing, be as ethical and above-board as you can. Bad-mouthing your ex-employer or work may make you feel good in the short-term, but it only serves to keep you focused on the past and not moving forward in a positive way. If you must, find one discreet person that you trust and vent to them. But limit yourself to that. Spreading your frustrations around the workplace, your friends and family can make you lose credibility and momentum. Remember, too, that venting through email, an online messaging system or in a bathroom stall may soon be broadcast and can provoke nasty feelings towards you. Even if your sentiments are right on the money, you risk ending up as a career wallflower or the woman who never gets to rectify her regrets.

**Make it amicable**
How you leave, even under less-than-ideal circumstances such as being fired, can make a big difference to how you're perceived in the future. While it's important to consider settlements or severance if you are let go, it's also important to behave ethically and with dignity. One way to

## ♥ Career Cupid ♥

ease the transition, whether you're leaving voluntarily or not, is to ask for an exit interview. This meeting allows you to ask and answer questions of your employer and can pave the way for a future positive reference and allow you to take away valuable information about your performance that you can use going forwards.

**Take out your wish list**
Whether you did the leaving or you were summarily ripped out of a job you thought was yours forever, it's time to refocus on the future. Think about what you have learned from the situation. Ask people you trust to honestly assess your strengths and weaknesses. Buy yourself a really expensive pair of congratulatory or conciliatory shoes. Use your knowledge to adapt your wish list so that you can start heading towards career happiness again.

# Chapter 14
# The seven-year itch

Even though you're content enough with your career life, you are still vulnerable to feeling itchy for new things. After all, you're a woman. Women change their minds. It's part of our genetic fabric along with the ability to drive and put on mascara simultaneously. Okay, some of us are better at that than others, but you get the idea.

Part of the secret to finding career Happily Ever After is to recognize when it's your own demons getting in the way. Even if you have found what you love to do and are doing it, there can come a time when the courtship and honeymoon phases have become a distant memory. Sure you're happy enough but there's a kind of "sameness" to your happiness that has become, well, a little dull. The seven-year itch is a chasm just waiting for you to yawn your way into.

**Expect the itch**
No, you don't need to go running out on one of those embarrassing trips to the nearest drugstore but you do need to focus on calming the itch. How? You do this first by expecting it to happen. Once you find your happy place at work, you probably think, "Oh, that itch thing could never happen to me". Even though denial is sometimes a woman's best friend – otherwise how would any of us cope with things like parallel parking or broken thing-a-ma-bobs on the whatchamacallits – I recommend facing the seven-year itch proactively.

**Fear not the itch**
Even the happiest of marriages sometimes reaches a stage where things need a little reenergizing. Experiencing the itch in a romantic relationship doesn't mean that you're a bad person or the other person isn't the right person. (Although if you're regularly finding that you would rather clean under the kitchen sink than have a conversation with your guy, you may need to take action.) Experiencing the itch in your dream job doesn't mean you should bail out immediately and start looking for something else. But ignore it at your peril. It will eat away at your career happiness while you're not looking (unless you feed it regularly with cake and then it just gets overweight and self-deprecating). It is something to pay attention to and for the worst-case-scenario-lovers amongst you, to plan for.

# ♥ Career Cupid ♥

### Schedule a date night

As you transition from honeymoon to married life, you may be thinking that nothing can touch your happiness. It can feel like a traitorous act when you try to plan for the future by setting up a regimented event like a date night. And even though it's hard for you to believe that there might come a time when you and your hunky won't be spending ten minutes saying goodbye to each other on the phone anymore, a date night is still a good initiative to start early.

At work, the same holds true. When you find a great job where you feel so comfortable and fulfilled, it's easy to leap right in to the day-to-day life and forget about consciously taking care of the career relationship. But a few years down the road, after hard slogging at something you admittedly loved, you may be wondering where all the fun went. If you start from the beginning by organizing a date night, you will have habits in place that will help you as you near the precipice of the seven-year itch.

### What does a career date night look like?

A career date night is different for everyone. The main idea is that it is a conscious appointment you make for yourself to focus on your career. Find what works for you and your career.

### *Some suggestions might include:*

- Finding a mentor you admire in your field and meeting that person once a month for dinner or coffee to gain inspiration and advice.

- Continuing your education in the field. Taking courses that will build your knowledge not only keeps you abreast of current trends but it also helps to revitalize your work energy.

- Organize a regular social gathering of colleagues where you blow off steam and appreciate each other as people.

- Cross-pollinate with similar organizations or work. Invite them to learn about what you do. Peek into what they do. See where you dove-tail.

- Attend seminars, conferences or listen to speakers to help you get reinspired and refocused on the work you do.

- Volunteer or work at one-time events to help you gain appreciation for what you do and to tap into more interests and skills you may want to fold into your work in the future.

Whatever your career date nights look like, it is important to treat them with care. Primp a bit before hand so you feel great. Choose activities that you love to do so that they don't simply feel like another obligation. Make time for them so that they become something you value and look forward to. Career date nights can lead to long-term happiness as they inject a little fire into your already happy work.

### Are you a career floosie?

I have a friend who admitted to me a few years ago that he only loves the beginnings of relationships. He needs the constant rush of infatuation and lives for the thrill of learning about a new person. Once it gets beyond that, he feels incredibly bored and frustrated. And yes, I think he's had more than his share of nasty messages on his answering machine!

Although you may not have this trait in your romantic relationships, ask yourself if it exists in your career relationships. For the generally career-itchy person, this can be a hard quality to face. Some people find many dream jobs, but when they get them, they can't be faithful. A friend of mine calls herself a "career floosie" because she flits from one thing to the next quite happily. You might too – although I totally understand if you don't want to use my friend's description for yourself. Bottom line is that if you are feeling itchy in your dream job, take a hard look at yourself. Make some decisions about what career Happily Ever After means to you. More on this in the last chapter of this book but suffice it to say that you need to figure out if you're feeling the seven-year itch or if this is just par-for-the-course in your unique career life.

### Don't worry, be happy

I only mention this because I succumb to the "Eeyore" syndrome on the odd occasion. There I am, tossing and turning in bed (I'd have insomnia except I love sleeping way too much), worrying about things. In the clear light of day as I am chugging caffeine and wondering why I slept so badly, I realize suddenly that I'm aspiring to live a movie life. In movie life, things are perfect. All the little problems and obstacles are gathered up neatly in this alluring package called a happy ending. I am so indoctrinated in the ways of happy endings. Orphans who find loving families. Shy, awkward women who find their Prince Charming. It's hokey and overly sentimental and the trouble is that in real life, life goes on after the happy endings. So it's not perfect. It can still be happy. Yet sometimes I find myself focusing on the relatively insignificant negatives – such as the tedium of doing monthly statistics or the rare client who is rude and entitled – and blowing them up so that they overshadow the overwhelmingly positive big picture. Ask yourself if you do the same thing. Maybe you're so used to having something to complain about that you are making your whole job seem like that movie where your

# ♥ Career Cupid ♥

favourite movie star got ugly to try to win an Oscar. Don't worry. They're still pretty underneath! In all likelihood, so is your job.

**Seek professional help if needed**
This bit might seem like a bit of good old-fashioned self-promotion but really it's just a happy coincidence. I'm going to suggest that when the going gets rough, you might want to seek professional advice. If talking to your girlfriends, mother, spouse, hairdresser or checkout guy at the grocery store isn't helping, check online or in your phone book for a professional who works with people on career issues. Sometimes a neutral party can help you suddenly and quite quickly get clarity on confusion. They are usually more blunt and direct than your loved ones, possibly due to the fact that they aren't going to want to ask you to have sex or a yoga date later.

**Buy the goop!**
You feel the itch. You know it's there. Yet you still persist in telling yourself that nothing is wrong. Before you know it, you've got a full-blown infection – all because you didn't want to take action and buy the goop at the drug store. The moral of this chapter is to understand that the seven-year itch exists, even in the best of jobs. The good news is that you can weather it happily. You can take responsibility for finding solutions proactively and do the things required to help you transition through it successfully. No one else is going to buy the goop for you. You have to take a deep breath and take it up to the cash register yourself. Don't worry. The teenage sales clerk desperately attempting to grow his first moustache has seen it all before.

♥ **Chapter 15** ♥

# Heeding the call of Career Cupid

As you reach the end of this book, you might be thinking, "Is this it? Has Career Cupid abandoned me? Where is my Happily Ever After?" And this, dear reader, is what might be the last chance for me to connect career Happily Ever After with romantic Happily Ever After.

When you fell in love with Hunky McHunkster from the volleyball team you play with on Wednesday nights even though he was totally taken, you probably weren't too happy with old Cupid. Cupid, as you know, can be a crafty little character who doesn't always seem to be on your side. But Cupid does have a way of keeping life interesting. Sometimes the experiences hurt and other times they are just so glorious that you find yourself jumping up and down gleefully and high five-ing the air in a very Celine-Dion-pounding-her-chest kind of manner. Yep, Cupid is a wise one and I for one certainly wouldn't want to live a life without the peaks and valleys – despite the occasional heartache and doldrums. So, just in case you were distracted by the crunching sound your double-stuffed Oreo cookies were making as you were reading, here are Cupid's lessons from each chapter.

**Finding career Happily Ever After is like dating**
It's messy, it's fun and at times it will scare the panties right off you. It's also practically essential to the plan of ever finding Happily Ever After. Have you ever met anyone who met their sweetheart by not going anywhere, not talking to anyone (even electronically) and without telling anyone anything about themselves? Unless you're in an arranged marriage, it's pretty rare. FYI – arranged careers are quite rare these days too. Despite this, many people I've worked with continue to have a huge desire for one so if you're longing for one right now, you're not alone.

If you've never done it before or haven't done it in a long time, the prospect of career dating might have you shaking in your strappy sandals. But getting out there and becoming visible is one of the best ways to help you find your dream work. Until they invent the much-anticipated "Boys 'R Us", think of career dating as something like going to the produce section of the local grocery store to meet men. It might feel ridiculous at first, but it's worked for lots of people! And, as the folks at Nike say, sometimes you should "just do it".

# ♥ Career Cupid ♥

**Sometimes you'll choose bad work**
Yep, you're sitting there looking at what you thought was your dream job lying on the couch with dirty old track pants and the remote permanently welded to its hand. You've lost that loving feeling and you somehow got into this situation without even being able to blame your mother!

Even if it's not Friday afternoon at the end of your long week, don't be afraid to keep believing in Happily Ever After. It does exist. But you won't find it if you sit there complaining about track-pant-job all weekend long instead of starting to take some action. It's time to take stock. What have you gained in this situation (there's always something despite how discouraging things may appear) and what can you carry with you (no, not office supplies, silly!) into your next step? Start preparing for some career dating, One-night Stands and even a transition job. Think of all the cute new jobs you'll meet!

**There's always an excuse to go shopping**
On the path to Happily Ever After, you always want to look your best. Who knows when dream guy or dream job will show up? Hopefully it's not on the day when you're wearing the skirt you found rumpled in the bottom of your closet that you can still fit into as long as you don't eat any lunch and survive on diet soda all day. You want to feel fabulous when the planets start to align! Bearing some general rules in mind, dress in a way that lifts your spirits and forwards your career. Remember, as long as your bank account allows, there's always time to engage in some retail therapy, especially when it makes you feel like the right person for your dream job.

**Noodles are vital in the lasagna-making process**
You are a woman and that means that you are complicated and layered. Possibly you are also prone to changing your mind. Taking responsibility for and keeping track of the joys and annoyances of your working life can feel onerous at times but it's really important.

It is really, really tempting to want to rush right into career dating so you can get to the grand prize = dream job soon! However, just like rushing into romantic dating, it works better if you know a few things about yourself first.

Whether you have gathered a little bit of life experience or a lot, spending some time working on your Hootchie Mama and wish lists is vital to finding Happily Ever After. This is the chapter not to skip because, just like the process of making lasagna, if you haven't spent time learning about and focusing a bit on all those layers you've got hiding under your "throws like a girl" exterior, you're likely to end up

♥ Chapter 15 ♥

with a bit of a soupy mess. Those lasagna noodles, though interpreted by some as a bit dull on their own, are crucial to the perfection of the finished dish.

### One-night Stands do not a career floosie make
Yep, it's finally true. You get to be a fancy-pants, social butterfly career floosie after all those years of behaving yourself. AND it will help you towards Happily Ever After. Huh, if only those people had told you this when you were a teenager!

Just remember that we're talking about Career One-night Stands, Speed Dating and Transition Guys and not the Hollywood version of *"Voulez vous coucher avec moi?"* Your goal is to make enjoyable contact with many, many people. Then love 'em and leave 'em, sister. Vengeance for grade nine's Tommy Smithers will be yours even more if you record your encounters in your little black (networking) book. But try to restrain yourself from reading it out loud to all your friends like he did, okay?

### Preparation is key when meeting his parents
Stay calm, but do not underestimate the importance of the interview. Every conversation you have with a potential employer (or mother-in-law) is an opportunity to showcase how much you love the work (or mother-in-law's son) and demonstrate why you are the woman who is right for the long-term role.

Remember to be authentically enthusiastic about her meatloaf without gushing to the point of sounding fake. This is the time to showcase your genuine interest in the work and convince the employer of your choice that you are the right choice for their beloved job. It's also the time for you to assess whether you can feel good about committing to this relationship. Listen to the clanging sounds going off in your gut – it may be that they're not just a result of the meatloaf.

### A dolphin proposal is not to be taken lightly
When you're in the enviable position to be offered what looks like a happily-ever-after job, take the time to pause and think about your decision. Just because hundreds of chlorine-happy eyeballs are staring at you, doesn't mean you should rush things.

Go back to your Hootchie Mama statements and check to see if you have strayed from your authentic place. Check your wish list to see if this opportunity really matches a good number of items you were looking for. There will be inevitable compromise of course, but the important thing here is to feel excited and happy about the future. If you accept a job and then walk around with a sinking feeling, your dolphin

♥ *Career Cupid* ♥

proposal may be weighing you down. And you know dolphins hate that. They're sensitive, friendly creatures who only want to help!

**Aim for a life of manageable torment**
Yeah, it stinks sometimes to be ethical. In fact, I often tell myself that I seem to be an outdated. goody-two-shoes when it comes to ethics and morals. Still, I think that most people would like to think of themselves as honourable, so trying to avoid cheating is a goal I think we can all agree on. When you're feeling bitter and twisted, lonely and abandoned or just plain bored, cheating can be hard to resist. And hey, we're talking about a JOB here not even a person. But cheating on the job really is cheating on a person. You're cheating on yourself – not to mention the people who rely on you and trust you. But you can resist falling into the cheating trap. Think about all the gorgeous shoes you didn't buy and the yummy calories you didn't eat. You have willpower up the wazoo! Just don't torment yourself for too long – we all have our breaking point so it's important to be taking steady action to get out of your temptation zone and on to bigger and better things.

**Resist the inexorable pull of going baggy**
Your life is unbelievably busy and the last thing you need is one more thing to think about. Going baggy isn't a derogatory comment that insinuates that you should look like a supermodel 24–7. It is supposed to remind you that you are worth caring about and that your Happily Ever After at work is worth pursuing and dreaming about.

Going baggy is a symptom of giving up. It signals that you are losing your ability to believe that new and exciting things are possible. It tells your job "you're not really worth bothering about anymore".  And just like men, jobs notice when you stop trying for them.

There will be times when you need to coast a bit. Every one and every job has a bit of an ebb and flow to it. In times of change, you are the one constant in your life and often – so is the work you do. Don't take it for granted. It can feed you when you're broke, it can motivate you when you're drifting. Make it a goal to keep putting effort in to your career relationship so that it can grow and inspire you. Treat it with respect and admiration and you can come out the other side still friends.

**You can love him but not be "in love" with him**
Despite my perhaps annoying belief in happy endings, there are times when a relationship just won't work anymore and the best thing for all concerned is for it to end. Getting out without getting bitter is a goal worth aiming for. So is keeping the relationship as amicable as possible

♥ Chapter 15 ♥

while you're giving back the keys and putting the contents of your desk drawers in a box.

Whether the divorce was of your choosing or not, leaving with dignity and your references intact will allow you to move on faster and with fewer conciliatory bottles of your favourite Merlot. Maybe you're not one of those mythical women who can split up with an ex and still be friends years later. Let's face it, we all think that's a little weird anyway. But it's something to aspire to in your career.

**Your Happily Ever After is unique to you**
No job, just like no man, will be completely perfect. Despite that rather gloomy-sounding fact, you can still live Happily Ever After at work. Each person finds her own definition of what Happily Ever After means in her life. For some people, it will be a stable job with fun coworkers and reasonable time off to spend on other pursuits. For others, it will be interesting, challenging, soul-fulfilling work that "completes" you.

Sometimes we get trapped in very all-or-nothing thinking. "I can't do this job forever!" No one said you had to do it forever – but maybe it's the right thing to do for now. If it helps you build a skill you didn't have before, helps you get contacts and references, helps you gain knowledge about what aspects of work are a good match for you and what kinds of environments you like, then you're not wasting your time. If you can avoid cheating and going baggy, you're investing in the building blocks that will help you get to more fulfilling options that are closer to your ideal.

One of the lessons of life, and this book, is that part of finding career happiness is being able to harness and savour the good stuff as it is happening. Even if you're not in the perfect job, it may be the perfect job for right now. And your life will be a lot more fun and less stressful if you can choose to pay more attention to the good stuff than the bad. This will free up a bunch of energy for going after and attracting your dream work.

When I got married, my maid of honour read a speech in which she said, "I don't believe in Happily Ever After, but the bride does and now she's found it." I realized, not for the first time that Happily Ever After is defined differently by everyone. You have a decision to make. It may be that you are not the long-term career relationship, happily-ever-after kind of a girl. Maybe you're a serial monogamist or more of a one-night stand type. Maybe that's your career Happily Ever After.

But whatever form your Happily Ever After takes at work, treat the search like a romance. It will be way more interesting and even fun! Like any romance, some of it is about a little luck and timing. A lot of it is about knowing yourself, having a wish list and finding the matches

# Career Cupid

that exist, even if they feel few and far between. Just like true love Happily Ever After, career Happily Ever After won't always be easy to find. Your journey may have its up and downs, just like any good romance. And if, like my maid of honour, you don't believe in Happily Ever After, it will exist in a different way for you. You will ultimately find the career happiness that suits you, as long as you keep on believing that it exists. And while you're on your way to it, I will be here rooting for you – and for all of us Happily Ever After girls – all the way.

# Lipstick, Business Letters and other Tools of the Trade

Useful information for your journey to Happily Ever After

## ♥ Chapter 16 ♥
# I need a vacation when . . .

Remember, this is the place where you write down the clues that you won't be able to see when you're over-worked, under-appreciated, over-tired and a whole bunch of other stressful-sounding words. So be honest.

**Some examples to get you started**
I know I need a vacation (or to take action on my career hunt for Happily Ever After) when:

- I feel tired all the time and/or people who used to count themselves among my friends tell me that I look tired all the time
- I find myself yelling "Yay, it's Friday!" six times before 8 a.m.
- I have started to rely on the psychic hotline to tell me if I should go to work or call in sick

Try to put items on your "I need a vacation" list that aren't really "I'm actually way past needing a vacation and am verging on a nervous breakdown" items. We don't want you to get that far down in the pit of despair before you start taking action.

♥ Chapter 17 ♥
# Test your dress code savvy – Answers

**Answers to the test on page 45**

**1. You should always wear a suit to an interview**

**FALSE** Unless you're going to a really corporate environment, it's probably not necessary to wear a really formal suit. Generally, something in the business casual category of dress will suffice for most interviews. However, just like a first date, being a little over-dressed shows you're genuinely interested and not just going out because your mother's bridge buddy fixed you up with her nephew.

**2. It's best to wear black, navy or grey so you'll be taken seriously**

**FALSE** Keeping in mind the work environment, wear colours that you feel good in and suit you. You may want to leave your cargo pants and neon orange sweater at home but they're getting overexposed anyway, right?

**3. Jeans are okay to wear to an interview as long as the workplace is casual or if you would normally be wearing a uniform**

**FALSE** After 20 years in the military, jeans are my husband's new uniform of choice, but even he can be pried out of them for an interview. Avoid wearing them to meet with employers. The possible exception might be if you are interviewing to be staff at a jeans store, in which case, I say, lucky you! (See earlier note on avoiding dreaded tapered jeans, page 41.)

**4. It's important to avoid wearing perfume to an interview**

**TRUE** Unless you're really up on your CPR and First Aid, you should never wear perfume to an interview. Many people are allergic and many organizations have instituted fragrance-free policies. The department store perfume counters are still pouting but they shouldn't worry. As long as there is dating (the romantic kind), there will be a market for fragrance.

♥ *Career Cupid* ♥

**5. Wear clothes that make your feel comfortable to an interview**

**TRUE**  Yep. It's a fact. You'll perform better and be less likely to make an employer worry about why you keep fidgeting if you wear clothes that feel comfortable. Remember to check for annoying, itchy tags so you don't have to squirm and ask for antihistamines in the middle of your interview.

**6. It's okay to borrow clothes to go to an interview**

**TRUE**  Hey, we can't all have Donald Trump's money (and thankfully, we don't have his hair!) Borrowing clothes is just fine as long as it's from someone whose clothes will fit you. I personally like to choose someone who has better fashion sense than me. Then I not only look professional, but I can go and visit my mother afterwards and she'll think that I'm finally getting my act together.

**7. If you have dyed your hair orange, you should dye it a more "normal" colour before an interview**

**FALSE**  You don't have to compromise your hair colour for a job . . . but if months are passing and you still have no job, you may need to consider whether your hair colour is having a negative impact on your search. If people point and laugh when you arrive for the interview, there's a good chance that your hair is a barrier . . . not just a colour never found in nature.

**8. What you say is more important than what you wear**

**TRUE**  If you can still remember high school when you read this, then it will probably seem like a completely different world than the one you lived through – where, in most cases, what you wear was THE most important thing. But when interviewing, it's more important for the employer not to be distracted by what you wear because they want to hear what you have to say. Who would have thought it?

**9. If you're just dropping off an application, you don't have to dress up**

**FALSE**  Maybe you're thinking, "I'll only be seeing the secretary or part-time bike messenger when I drop off my application, so why should I dress up?" In many cases, you're right, but the part people forget is that those people have eyes and opinions and connections to the boss. Many employers will ask their staff for

♥ Chapter 17 ♥

an opinion of the people who drop off applications. So dust yourself off a bit and make a good first impression – no matter who it's with. Then treat your gussied-up self to a latte at the coffee shop where the cute barista works every Thursday.

**10. You should never wear white after Labour Day**

**FALSE**   Who made up that dumb rule anyway? I personally avoid wearing white all the time because it seems to court clumsiness and disasters but hey, if you love white, I think the rules now say you can now wear it willy-nilly. Whew. That's a relief! I hate it when my ability to spill spaghetti sauce on white pants on New Year's Eve is hampered by some silly rule.

♥ Chapter 18 ♥
# Speed dating cheat sheet

When you're ready to begin Speed Dating and One-night Stands, it's sometimes helpful to have a bit of script for talking on the telephone or writing a letter or email to introduce yourself. (See Chapter 7 for the whole deal on the reasons why this is a good idea.)

**Telephone example**

"Hello, Mr/Ms So-and-so. My name is Lily Vanilly and I learned about your organization through the *Directory of Pigs & Whistles*. I'm not looking for a job but I'm really very interested in the work you do as a Roller Skate Mechanic. I'm wondering if it would be possible to talk to you for 10 or 15 minutes some time, at your convenience, about what you do day-to-day?"

**Email or letter example**

Mr/Ms So-and-so
Roller Skate Mechanic
Joe's House of Tiny Wheels
456 Penny Lane
Fabulousville
Fabuloso
ph: (111) 555-8989

Dear Mr/Ms So-and-so

Ever since I was a child, I have loved roller skating. I currently work as a baker but I am nearly ready to go after my dream of training to become a roller skate mechanic. I am not looking for a job right now but I am looking for information about the work of roller skate mechanics. I have heard that you are among the best in your arena and I wonder if you would be willing to chat with me soon, at your convenience, for ten or fifteen minutes. I would be very interested in finding out more about what it's really like to be a roller skate mechanic.

# ♥ Career Cupid ♥

I'll call you in a week or so to ensure that you received this email/letter and to set up a time that is convenient for you to talk about your work.

Many thanks for considering this. I know how busy you are and I really appreciate any short time you can spare.

Sincerely


Ms Fabuloso Career Speed Dater
123 Promenade Square
Brilliance
New Brilliance
Ph: (222)-555-5656

# Acknowledgements

A writer needs sustenance and mine is a well-honed combination of chocolate and reading for inspiration. I have been inspired and humbled by the writing of Antoine de Saint Exupéry, Jennifer Weiner, Michael Fader, Greta and Janet Podleski, David E. Kelley, Lucy Maud Montgomery, Steve Krug, Warren Zevon, Sue Monk Kidd, Marie-Louise Gay, Heather Huebner, Mark Knopfler, Astrid Lindgren, Grigg Veley, Jaclyn Moriarty, Amy Sherman-Palladino, Sophie Kinsella, Arlo Guthrie, Dr. Seuss, Heather O'Neill and so many more. Not all those people are famous yet, but they should be.

Thank you to Elizabeth Croft, who took up the Career Cupid quest with speed and enthusiasm even though there was a black bear on the loose in her neighbourhood. Thanks also to Marilyn Inglis, who edited expertly, gently and quickly – longitude and latitude notwithstanding.

A day without my 1973 Volkswagen Beetle, "Daizybug", feels like a day flying without my superhero cape. I want to thank the person who found Daizy for me and convinced me to live one of my lifelong dreams. You can call him "Car Cupid".

Thank you to my colleagues, past and present at Career Services and Queen's University. You daily – and mostly thanklessly – support students on their roads to career Happily Ever After. Despite all the Gaelic stuff that I still don't completely understand, you have kept me entertained for many years now. For someone with hot feet like me, that's saying something.

I am afraid of many things. Cows, hairdressers, and revolving doors are a few that jump to mind. Since the list is far more extensive than those three items, I have known since childhood that I was never going to be a free spirit. More like a free-range chicken. Then, along came a friend's mom who described me as "fearless". For a cow/hairdresser/revolving-door 'fraidy cat like me, that was a statement to live up to. Thank you, Whit and Dot.

To my family who has stoked the fires of humour, word smithing, self-deprecation, grammar and ambition. Thank you for fat pills, leathers, Zzzzz, and the rest of the Bardon/Fleming vernacular that has entertained me over the years.

I heard once that the average one-year-old smiles hundreds of times a day and the average adult smiles less than ten. Thank you to all my

♥ Career Cupid ♥

kindred spirit friends who help me exceed the statistics every day: Freckles, Taller Bloke, U.O.S. Guy, Katerooski, Hemingway, Snow White, Flaming Orange Girl, Bamboo Guy and Kitegirl.

Most of all, I want to thank Michael for clever puns, persistent gallantry and unwavering, unconditional gushy stuff. Our Happily Ever After first inspired this book.

# About the Author

Christine Fader has worked as a Career Counsellor at Queen's University since 1998 and also provides career and medical school admission coaching through Careercupid.com. Christine has twice edited the best-selling campus book, *Queen's Best Résumés and Cover Letters*. Her articles have been featured on Workopolis.com, Schoolfinder.com, in the *Globe and Mail*, and career-focused magazines. Christine speaks frequently about career management at conferences and events and has developed and taught customized career classes for over 10 years. She has been a qualified MBTI™ practitioner since 1999 and a member of the Canadian Association of Career Educators and Employers (CACEE) since 1998. In her spare time, Christine likes to use medical terminology, eat tomatoes and drive her 1973 Volkswagen Beetle.

# More titles in the Canadian Career Series

**So You Want to Be a Lawyer, Eh?**
by Adam Letourneau B.Sc., B.A., LL.B

**So You Want to Be a Doctor, Eh?**
by Dr. Anne Berndl M.D., B.Sc.H

**So You Want to Be a Pilot, Eh?**
by James Ball, B.A., CPL

Do you have great career advice to offer and writing experience? Writing On Stone Press is accepting proposals for career related titles. We are looking for submissions about careers in:

- Architecture
- Nursing
- Dentistry

And more. See our website for details.
www.writingonstone.ca

WRITING
ON STONE
PRESS